Free Will Baptist Doctrines

J. D. O'Donnell

Randall House Publications
P.O. Box 17306
114 Bush Road
Nashville, Tennessee 37217

Table of Contents

1

The Holy Scriptures

BACKGROUND

Today, instead of the unbelieving world attacking the Bible, there are many who call themselves Christians who deny that the Bible is the inspired Word of God. Many are proclaiming from the pulpits and in printed material that the Bible is full of myths; that it contains much that is in error; that perhaps it contains the Word of God; but each individual must decide for himself what portion speaks to him and his experience. Free Will Baptists, along with all conservatives, fundamentalists, evangelicals (choose the preferred name!), believe that the Bible is the inspired Word of God, ". . . the Old and New Testaments; . . . written by holy men, inspired by the Holy Spirit. . . . They are a sufficient and infallible rule and guide to salvation and all Christian worship and service" (*Treatise*). They are without error in their original form.

In order to understand the doctrine of inspiration, one must look at the meaning of the word *inspire*. The word comes from two Greek words: *theos*, which means God, and *penin*, which means to breathe. The term in 2 Timothy 3:16, "given by inspiration," means that the Old Testament writings resulted from God breathing into the authors that which they wrote. Inspiration, then, is the act of

God as He speaks through men, and the result is the same as if He spoke these utterances with His own lips. This is true whether the words were spoken or written. God is the author.

When there were available sources, God directed the writers to these sources. When there were no available human sources, God (Himself) gave the writers the needed information.

All of the books of the Old Testament, as accepted by Protestants, were in existence during the life of Christ. Jesus referred to and endorsed these as the Scriptures in His day. We have the testimony of the early church writers as to the New Testament books. None of the Apocrypha is included. There is nothing to disprove any of the New Testament as being part of the Holy Scriptures. Space will not permit a long discussion of the canonicity of the Scriptures. The reader is referred to *How We Got the Bible* by Neil R. Lightfood for a thorough study of this subject.

A teacher will find it profitable to spend some time in independent study of the canonizing of our Scriptures. He will gain a greater appreciation of how God has preserved His Word throughout the centuries.

When the statement is made that the Bible is free from error in its original manuscripts, it is not inferred that all of the versions are without mistake. The versions are composed from copies. No one knows of any originals in existence. But a close comparison of the ancient manuscripts will reveal that there is remarkably close agreement. The full message of God's Word has been preserved, and men have proved that they can rely on it. It is good to remember Christ's own words, "My word shall never pass away."

OUTLINE

I. **The Old Testament Is the Word of God (2 Peter 1:15-21)**

II. **The New Testament Is the Word of God (2 Timothy 3:14-17)**

INTRODUCTION

In introducing this lesson on the Holy Scriptures, or the Holy Bible, let the words of Henry Halley be noted:

"Everybody ought to love the Bible. Everybody ought to Read the Bible. Everybody. It is God's Word. It holds the Solution of Life. It tells about the Best Friend mankind ever had, the Noblest, Kindest, Truest Man that ever trod the earth.

"It is the Most Beautiful Story ever told. It is the Best Guide to human conduct ever known. It gives a Meaning, and a Glow, and a Joy, and a Victory, and a Destiny, and a Glory, to Life elsewhere unknown.

"Most people, in their serious moods, must have some wonderment in their minds as to how things are going to stack up when the End comes. Laugh it off, toss it aside, as we may, THAT DAY WILL COME. And THEN WHAT? Well, it is the Bible that has the answer. And an unmistakable answer it is. There is a God. There is a Heaven. There is a Hell. There is a Saviour. There will be a Day of Judgment. Happy the man, who, in the days of his flesh, makes his peace with the Christ of the Bible, and gets himself ready for the Final Take-Off.

"How can any thoughtful person keep his heart from warming up to Christ, and to the Book that tells about Him? Everybody ought to love the Bible. Everybody. EVERYBODY!" (*Halley's Bible Handbook*, page 805).

Free Will Baptists place the doctrine of the Scriptures in a lofty place in their *Treatise*. Because a proper attitude toward the Scriptures determines attitudes toward all the basic doctrines, it is placed first. To believe that the Scriptures are the Word of God, that they contain God's revelation of Himself to man, lays a foundation for one's faith in the deity of Christ, His atonement for men's sins, and Heaven as a reward for those who believe in Christ. If one does not revere the Scriptures but sees them as merely

3

human writings, he has no foundation for faith or authority for his life. Study carefully these Scriptures in regard to the Word of God and also study the section in the *Free Will Baptist Treatise* in regard to the Scriptures.

I. THE OLD TESTAMENT IS THE WORD OF GOD (2 Peter 1:15-21)

While some groups have taken a light view of the Old Testament, Free Will Baptists believe that the Holy Scriptures are composed of the "Old and New Testaments." In 2 Peter 1:15-21 Peter gives us a look at his deep respect for the Old Testament. These verses show the closeness of the two testaments. Peter is giving witness to the facts revealed in the New Testament and declares that they are true because he and others were "eyewitnesses of his majesty" (verse 16). But then to further prove their claims he points to something even more convincing than these eyewitness accounts. This is the Old Testament which contains "a more sure word of prophecy" (verse 19).

These verses from 2 Peter were not intended as a sermon on the inspiration of the Scriptures. They are merely an aside thought into which Peter passed from dealing with other matters. However, they serve well as a basis for teaching the inspiration and reliability of the Old Testament.

Introducing these verses (verse 13), Peter told his readers that as long as he was "in this tabernacle" or still alive that he wanted "to stir you up by putting you in remembrance." However, this old eyewitness of the events in the life of the Lord knew that his days were numbered and that soon he would pass on into glory. In verse 15 he expressed the hope that before he died he would be able to put the things which he had seen into writing so that they would always be "in remembrance."

4

Tradition tells us that Peter was able to carry out this desire before his decease. The gospel of Mark is reported to be the gospel according to Peter. The tradition which has been handed down tells us that Peter reported the events of the life of Christ to John Mark and that he recorded them. It is very significant that several items in this gospel in regard to Peter are given greater clarity and detail in Mark than in the other gospels.

There are in existence certain books which reputedly tell of the boyhood days of Christ and other events in His life but do not have the ring of authority about them. Some of the stories told in these false writings (called apocryphal works) are very fanciful and sometimes silly. It may be that some of them were already in existence in Peter's day. This may be why he wrote that "we have not followed cunningly devised fables" (2 Peter 1:16). The Gnostics (a group of heretics of Jewish-Christian relation) of the second century had many fables and some of them may have already been developing at this early date. These "cunningly devised fables" were also basic to the religions of the heathen.

Peter was here referring to the "power and coming of our Lord Jesus Christ." Some have taken these words to refer to the Second Coming of Christ. The words *power* and *coming* do seem to refer to that event but do not necessarily mean that future coming. Actually, it seems more likely that he is referring to that first coming for he goes on to mention the Transfiguration at which time he and the other inner circle disciples beheld the glory of the Lord (Matthew 17:1-12).

A further evidence that he was speaking of that first coming is found in the fact that he and others "were eyewitnesses of his majesty." Peter, James, and John were with Jesus in the mountain when He "was transfigured before them: and his face did shine as the sun, and his raiment was white as the light" (Matthew 17:2). But Peter was not speaking of the Transfiguration as an isolated event. To him that was typical of His "power and coming." To Peter this event represented all the glory of that first coming of our Lord.

Describing that scene in the mountain, Peter said that Jesus "received from God the Father honour, in the voice which spoke to him: glory, in the light which shone from him." The demonstration of God in the light and the evidence of God in the voice were confirmation to an earthly witness of who Jesus was. God chose to bear witness to these selected men of the true nature of Jesus Christ so they could give special witness to others.

The term, "a voice to him from the excellent glory," is a sublime statement of this great event. The "excellent glory" may be referring to God Himself. Others take it to refer to Heaven or the bright cloud which overshadowed them (Matthew 17:5). This latter may be the more correct view since Matthew mentions "a voice out of the cloud." However, in the next verse, Peter mentions "this voice which came from heaven."

That voice of God out of the cloud gave a stamp of approval to all that Jesus had taught the disciples. It made valid that statement which Peter had confessed a few days earlier that "Thou art the Christ, the Son of the living God" (Matthew 16:16).

To further prove the fact which he has presented, Peter referred to the happening itself in verse 18 when he wrote, "This voice . . . we heard, when we were with him in the holy mount." A voice from Heaven is not the usual way God speaks to human beings. But on occasions when the situation needs such evidence from God, He does so let himself be heard. This was the second time that such a voice gave testimony to who Jesus was (Matthew 3:17). Once more, as He headed toward Jerusalem to accomplish the atonement, such a voice spoke from Heaven and gave such a witness (John 12:28).

It is in verse 19 that Peter comes to the real emphasis of this passage. Although Peter and the other disciples were witnesses to the ministry of Christ, there is one testimony which is stronger

than theirs. That is the "more sure word of prophecy." Peter is saying that in a comparison the prophetic Word of God contained in
the Old Testament is firmer and more secure than the word of eyewitnesses. To many there is a question how this could be so. The
answer for several reasons is simple: (1) Prophecy was a much
broader and larger witness than the witness of the apostles. It gave
a broader witness for it was the testimony of many more. (2) It was
a witness which preceded the event and which was made sure by
the actual event. Men over a span of several centuries gave a united witness to an event that took place as they had said. (3) The testimony of the apostles alone, with no other proof, could have
been a misunderstanding of what was reality. Groups of men have
been wrong before and since.

Peter urges his readers to take heed unto prophecy "as unto a
light that shineth in a dark place." What prophecy reveals is compared to a light shining in darkness. By this statement he does not
mean that they should just notice it, but that they should be obedient to what it reveals. They should recognize who Jesus is and
obey His Word "until the day dawn, and the day star arise in your
hearts." Peter was not talking to unsaved men and urging them to
take Christianity. He was talking to men of "like precious faith"
and begging them to heed the Word of Prophecy until their faith
was completed in a mature relationship with the Risen Lord.
There seems to be nothing that would make this refer to the
Second Coming.

Peter gives a caution in verse 20. Believers were to recognize
"that no prophecy of the scriptures is of any private interpretation." This has been interpreted to mean (1) that no prophecy can
be interpreted of itself without comparing it with others, (2) that
the prophets did not understand what they wrote, or (3) that the
prophecies have a hidden meaning that cannot be known from
the prophecy itself. The real meaning seems to be that the
prophets did not give the prophecies the meaning they desired

and neither should we attempt to stamp them with our particular beliefs. Each has a meaning given to it by God and our search should be to learn what God spoke through it.

This interpretation is borne out by the first phrase of verse 21, especially the first part. Peter said, "The prophecy came not in old time by the will of man." The Old Testament Scriptures were not of human origin. It is going too far to say that the prophets did not even understand what they spoke and wrote. Surely these men were lifted by the Spirit of God into an understanding of what they spoke. It is easy to believe that God revealed some parts of the future to the understanding of these men. How else would their anticipations of the Messiah and His work be explained? But the important thing is that the prophecy did not originate by their will.

The reality of the fact was that "holy men of God spake as they were moved by the Holy Ghost." This is one of the New Testament passages which teaches the inspiration of the Old Testament Scriptures. The real meaning of the statement is to say that the Old Testament writers spoke or wrote in their capacities as special agents of God. When they said, "Thus saith the Lord," they were speaking the message which God had given to them to deliver to men. It was only "as they were moved" or inspired that they would deliver such a message saying, "This is the very word of God."

The *Free Will Baptist Treatise* speaks on this point by stating: "They (The Holy Scriptures) were written by holy men, inspired by the Holy Spirit, and are God's revealed word to man." The very fact that they spoke as "they were moved by the Holy Ghost" made the origin of the message in God.

Believers need to recognize the difference between *revelation* and *inspiration*. When these two terms are used in regard to the Scriptures, it refers to that information in the Bible which came directly from God through the Holy Spirit and could not have been known or found out any other way. Although the Bible as a whole is the revelation from God of Himself to man, there are many items in it from man's experience, from genealogical tables, and other sources. Revelation in the strict sense refers to passages such as Genesis 1 or Isaiah 53, which had to come from God.

Inspiration concerns the writing down of the Scriptures. It was the movement of the Holy Spirit upon the writers of the Word of God that led them in the selection of materials to be included in the particular work of each. Both revelation and inspiration were the work of God moving men through the Holy Spirit.

Some false views of inspiration to be avoided by believers are these:

(1) The Bible is on a level with the holy writings of other religions. (2) The Bible contains some inspired materials but not all of it is of such a nature. (3) The Bible is a completely human production.

A true view of inspiration will teach that the Bible is all inspired, both the Old and New Testaments. It will hold that "the Holy Spirit of God so guided its original production as to secure it from error and omission." The belief in the full inspiration of the Bible is referred to as the *plenary-verbal* view of inspiration.

These verses written by Peter would not let us overlook an important fact. That is the use of both human and divine agencies in the production of the Scriptures. Stress has already been placed upon the work of God through the Holy Spirit guiding in the Scriptures' production. However, human agency was employed in their production as well. The word of prophecy came to us through an unknown number of men from Moses to Malachi. This covers a period of around one thousand years.

These "holy men of God" (2 Peter 1:21) came from many walks of life. Moses and Joshua were national leaders, David and Solomon were kings, Jeremiah and Ezekiel were prophet-priests, Daniel a statesman, Amos a shepherd and gatherer of sycamore fruit. The greater number were prophets, although the writers of several books were anonymous. They all bore one common likeness: they "spake as they were moved by the Holy Ghost."

The manner in which the Holy Spirit moved upon them is not specifically described. Gaussen explains inspiration as an "inexplicable power" (one that cannot be explained). Moses had direct confrontations (conversations) with God. Ezekiel heard God speak through visions as did Zechariah. The main means by which God has spoken to His people is through heart impressions. The "still, small voice" which spoke to Elijah was probably of this nature.

II. THE NEW TESTAMENT IS THE WORD OF GOD (2 Timothy 3:14-17)

When we say that the New Testament is the Word of God, we mean that it is that truth which God has revealed to man regarding Himself and salvation. The Old and New Testaments go together and are unique in that they are the only writing which can be referred to as the Word of God. What can be said of Old Testament revelation and inspiration can also be said for the New Testament.

These verses from Paul to Timothy in regard to the inspiration of the Holy Scriptures are speaking of the Old Testament instead of the New Testament. However, it wasn't long after Paul wrote his epistles before they were recognized on a par with the Old Testament Scriptures. Even Peter in his second epistle recognized Paul's writings on the same basis as other Scriptures. Notice what he said: "As our beloved brother Paul also according to the wisdom given unto him hath written unto you; as also in all his epistles, speaking in them of these things; in which are some things hard to be understood, which they that are unlearned and unstable wrest, as they do also the other scriptures, unto their own destruction" (3:15, 16). Thus we can say that what Paul recorded here about the Scriptures and their inspiration could also be applied to his writings.

Paul introduces these verses with the conjunction "but," which tells us that they are vitally related to what has just been said. This background is on the fact that "evil men and seducers shall wax worse and worse, deceiving, and being deceived" (2 Timothy 3:13). In both his epistles Paul warns Timothy against "teachers of the law" (1 Timothy 1:7) and "profane and vain babblings" (2 Timothy 2:16). These teachers were dealing in ". . . fables and endless genealogies, which minister questions, rather than godly edifying . . ." (1 Timothy 1:4). Their regard was for "words to no profit, but to the subverting of the hearers" (2 Timothy 2:14).

Rather than following these men, Timothy was warned to flee from them and "continue thou in the things which thou hast learned and hast been assured of" (2 Timothy 3:14). Timothy had an outstanding background in the area of Christian instruction before he attained his position at Ephesus. He had received a godly heritage through his grandmother Lois and his mother Eunice" (2 Timothy 1:5). As the "dearly beloved son" of Paul in the faith, he had started out early in a practical ministry and had been guided very carefully into the Scriptures by Paul. These were the three people from whom he had learned "these things." Observing their lives and seeing the Word exemplified gave him those things of which Paul said "thou . . . hast been assured of."

It was important for Timothy to remember "of whom thou hast learned them." Youth have a tendency to cast off the teachings of their elders. In this age of ours which threatens to throw off all restraints, our youth need to be encouraged to look at the ones who have taught them and to compare their lives with the lives of those who would lead them into error. These are those who "walk in the light, as he is in the light." Following these, one will not go astray.

Timothy was fortunate above most children for as Paul reminded him, "From a child thou hast known the holy scriptures" (verse 15). Knowledge always increases responsibility. This responsibility is great when a young person like Timothy is able to react to that responsibility and dedicate his energies toward its duties from an early age.

The Hebrew Law made provision for the training of youth in its precepts. Moses, voicing the command of God, had said: "These words, which I command thee this day, shall be in thine heart: And thou shalt teach them diligently unto thy children, and shalt talk of them when thou sittest in thine house, and when thou walkest by the way, and when thou liest down, and when thou risest up. And thou shalt bind them for a sign upon thine hand, and they shall be as frontlets between thine eyes. And thou shalt write them upon the posts of thy house, and on thy gates" (Deuteronomy 6:6-9). In Deuteronomy 11:19, 20 he wrote, "Ye shall teach them your children, speaking of them when thou sittest in thine house, and when thou walkest by the way, when thou liest down, and when thou risest up, and thou shalt write them upon the door posts of thine house, and upon thy gates." It was obedience to these commands which had brought young Timothy his knowledge of the Scriptures.

It is interesting to note that Paul, though speaking of the Old Testament Scriptures, wrote that they "are able to make thee wise unto salvation." Paul himself was well-versed in the Scriptures. He went for a long time blinded to the real truth, but finally all of his knowledge of the Scriptures aided him in a realization that Christ was the Messiah, the Son of God.

The means through which these make one wise unto salvation is "faith which is in Christ Jesus." Knowledge of the Scriptures alone is not sufficient for salvation. Writing of some who did not believe the Old Testament Scriptures, the writer of Hebrews wrote, "The word preached did not profit them, not being mixed with faith in them that heard it" (4:2; compare Romans 10:14).

In verse 16 of this lesson Paul gives us the classic statement on the inspiration of the Scriptures. Some translators have reduced the strength of his statement by rendering this passage other than its apparent intent. The *American Standard Version* (1901 edition) translates it, "Every scripture inspired of God." This was followed by the *New English Bible* which rendered it, "Every inspired scripture has its use." Both suggest that not all Scriptures are inspired. The *Authorized Version* translates the passage, "All scripture is given by inspiration of God." Even the *Revised Standard Version* gives it this sense with its translation which reads: "All scripture is inspired by God." Thus it sets forth the plenary view of the inspiration of the Holy Scriptures. *All*, the Bible in its entirety, is inspired.

The single Greek word here translated inspired of God is an expression and idea connected with the Holy Spirit. The word for *breath* and *spirit* are the same. Spirit comes from the concept that it is the breath of life. In this instance the word amounts to *inspired*. It suggests that the writers of Holy Scriptures were under the influence of God in their writing.

Because of its quality of inspiration each Scripture is "profitable for doctrine, for reproof, for correction, for instruction in righteousness." One point that is often missed here is the ones to whom these are profitable. The direction is usually pointed toward the student. But it is the teacher who is intended. It was Timothy, the youthful leader, who was being told that the Scriptures could be profitable to him.

The areas listed in which they can be profitable to the teacher are in doctrine, reproof, correction, and instruction in righteousness. *Doctrine* involves the communication of truth regarding divine things. It is the teaching of the truths of the gospel. *Reproof* is concerned with the convincing of those who would contradict the truth as presented in the gospel. It could concern the convincing of a man in regard to his sins, and the claims of Christ on his life. *Correction* refers to the great task of Timothy at Ephesus in refuting heretical doctrines which were creeping into the church. Paul had warned him about these law teachers and their damnable doctrines. The Word of God was the only useful instrument to correct their errors. "Instruction in righteousness" is a reference to the more practical aspects of the gospel. It is good to know the truth, to be convinced of its worth, and to be corrected in areas of wrong; but it is important to have instruction in how it applies to life. To know what is required of believers involves much instruction for new converts coming out of a worldly situation. New converts do not just automatically know how to put gospel principles in effect in their lives. They need instruction in those principles.

It is in verse 17 that the profitableness of the inspired Scriptures is summarized: "that the man of God may be perfect, throughly furnished unto all good works." Perfect here carries the concept of "ready at every point." Truly the man of God who has his "feet shod with the preparation of the gospel of peace; . . . and the sword of the Spirit, which is the word of God" (Ephesus 6:15-17) is well-equipped for facing the enemy. Such a man has the necessary foundation for his work and the ready weapon in his hand.

"Throughly furnished" can be translated "throughly made ready." It is in the area of the Word of God that the man of God has his special task. When he is equipped with the proper knowledge of the Word, his basic training for service is complete. The knowledge of the Word prepares any man of God for teaching and instructing others. But it also prepares him for "all good works." This regards every area of the spiritual life whether it be correction, reproof, doctrine, or areas of practical instruction in righteousness.

The high regard which the writers of the Holy Scriptures had for previously written Scriptures is the same high regard that all believers should have. The psalmist in Psalm 119 expresses his heart attitude in full reverence of the Word of God. We who now have the gospel of Jesus Christ added to the revered Old Testament have even greater reason to rejoice in the Scriptures which reveal God to us in the fullest sense.

2

God, His Existence and Attributes

BACKGROUND

Perhaps one of the most sublime portions of Scripture regarding the revelation of God is the nineteenth psalm. In this psalm it is shown that God is revealed in nature, in the Scriptures, and in the righteous life. These three witnesses are proof enough to the open mind that there is a God.

Although the atheist may try to give a rational explanation of nature and deny the Bible, he is faced with a difficult problem when he is called upon to explain the change in an individual whose life is transformed by the Lord Jesus Christ. As someone has said, "The Christian is the only Bible some people read."

Because God is "past finding out," there have been many attempts to explain Him. The attributes which have been used to describe God are men's feeble efforts to explain that which is unexplainable. To know God, however, is to become acquainted with His Son, Jesus Christ. "He that hath seen me hath seen the Father," said Jesus (John 14:9). And the writer of Hebrews concurs, "God, who at sundry times and in divers manners spake in time past . . . Hath in these last days spoken unto us by his Son . . ." (Hebrews 1:1, 2a).

OUTLINE

I. **The Existence of God (Deuteronomy 6:1-19)**
II. **The Nature of God (Deuteronomy 4:15-23)**
III. **The Attributes of God (Romans 1: 1-32)**

INTRODUCTION

During the "God Is Dead" controversy, this writer in a service, opened with the exclamation that "God is dead," and then proceeded to disclaim the theory. A little girl about four years old, sitting on the front row with her mother, heard only the emphatic saying, "God is dead!" Upon hearing it, she looked into her mother's face and asked, "Is He really, mother?"

If this controversy had no other effect, it did at least arouse some believers to the threat of liberal doctrines to the faith of our fathers. The new doctrine may have arisen because the church so ineffectively demonstrates that they serve the True and Living God. A dead faith in believers is always a testimony to the world that God is dead. If God is not alive in believers, the world has no reason to believe their testimony that He is in any way different from the idols of the world.

The approach in this lesson will be more topical than an exposition of the Scriptures given for the lesson. The facts of this outline are not presented in one definite area of Scriptures but must be gleaned from many. On beginning a study of the lesson, note first the statement from the *Free Will Baptist Treatise* stating the doctrine of God.

"The Scriptures teach that there is only one true and living God, who is Spirit, self-existent, eternal, immutable, omnipresent, omniscient, omnipotent, independent, good, wise, holy, just, and merciful; the Creator, Preserver, and Governor of the Universe; the Redeemer, Saviour, Sanctifier, and Judge of men; and the only proper object of worship.

"The mode of His existence, however, is a subject far above the understanding of man—finite beings cannot comprehend Him. There is nothing in the universe that can justly represent Him, for there is none like Him. He is the fountain of all perfection and happiness. He is glorified by the whole creation, and is worthy to be loved and served by all intelligence."

Although this statement does not cover all problems and views of the doctrine of God, it does give the basic picture of the character of God.

I. THE EXISTENCE OF GOD
(Deuteronomy 6:1-19)

One of the earliest facts that a Bible reader recognizes is that the Bible nowhere tries to prove the existence of God. Although it calls the man a fool who says, "There is no God" (Psalm 14:1; 53:1), it only assumes the existence of God from Genesis 1:1 and never sets forth any arguments to prove it. The Bible does argue that He is the only God in contrast to idols who are only vanities.

Those who deny the existence of the one true God fall into six classes: atheists, agnostics, pantheists, polytheists, dualists, and deists. The atheists deny the existence of God. There are those who deny the existence of God completely. Others are only practical atheists in that they are indifferent to God. Agnostics are those who deny the possibility of a knowledge of God. As far as they are concerned, there may be a God, but they do not believe that man can be certain.

The pantheistic view is that every thing that exists, whether material objects or mind, is derived from a single substance. The totality of all things is God. The materialistic pantheists teach that matter is the cause of all existence. Idealistic pantheism teaches that mind is the source of all things. Both deny a personal God. Dualism traces all things back to two distinct things which cannot be reduced. Some of them would even claim two gods or say that both God and matter (Satan) were eternal.

Polytheism, of course, is the view that there are many gods. This has been the philosophy which has been the foundation of most of the world's idolatry. Deism is the view which teaches that there is a God but that He does not reveal Himself to man. He is completely separate and apart from His creation and cannot be known by man.

Belief in God is learned by intuition. Paul tells us "that which may be known of God is manifest in them; for God hath shewed it unto them" (Romans 1:19). However, "when they [the heathen] knew God, they glorified him not as God, neither were thankful; but became vain in their imaginations, . . . And changed the glory of the uncorruptible God into an image made like to corruptible man" (verses 21, 23). In the next chapter he mentions "the work of the law written in their hearts" (2:15).

This religious element in man's nature has been found to be universal. Nowhere have there been large segments of any population which had any strong tendencies toward atheism. David Livingstone, one of the earliest white men to visit the heart of Africa, said, "The existence of God and of future life is everywhere recognized in Africa." The evidence for God is so plain that men everywhere accept His existence as a fact.

In Deuteronomy 6:4 begins what the Hebrews referred to as the Shema. This is merely the first Hebrew word of the passage which begins with "Hear." The Shema passage is not an argument for God. As other Scriptures it assumes there is a God. This fact is taken for granted and then it sets forth the unity of God: "The LORD our God is one LORD." The verse following this introductory remark gives a summation of what Jesus called the "first and great" commandment: to love God supremely with all of one's being.

Several good arguments have been set forth for the existence of God. These arguments are not independently proofs of God, but taken together the evidence is piled up and adds to man's inborn belief. The chief of these arguments are as follows:

1. *The Cosmological Argument* which states that everything must have a cause. The universe was begun; therefore, there must be a cause for its existence. Something near this basis for argument is set forth in Hebrews 3:4 which says: "Every house is builded by some man; but he that built all things is God."

2. *The Ontological Argument* which declares that the very concept of God is proof of His existence. The idea of a perfect being is arrived at by a reflection upon self. Augustine gave the classic statement of this concept when he said, "God is more truly thought than he is described, and exists more truly than he is thought." This means that man's idea of God is truer to what is reality than his description of Him is. Yet his expressed or unexpressed idea is less than what the reality is.

3. *The Teleological Argument* teaches that the "order and useful arrangement in a system imply intelligence and purpose in the originating cause; the universe is characterized by order and useful arrangement; therefore, the universe has an intelligent and free cause." In Psalm 94:9 the psalmist wrote: "He that planted the ear, shall he not hear? he that formed the eye, shall he not see?"

4. *The Moral Argument* shows how that conscience is evidence of the fact of obedience or disobedience of a moral law. This implies a lawgiver. This must be God. Also involved is the recognition of the inequality between the happiness of good men and bad men on earth. There must be a hereafter in which an almighty arbiter will judge inequalities among men.

5. *The Argument from Congruity* is based on the belief that a theory which best explains related facts is probably true. A belief in

God is the best explanation for our mental, moral, and religious nature; therefore God must exist.

It is important for man to have a proper knowledge of what God is. Philosophers and liberals in religion have called Him "the eternal mind" (Plato), "the Absolute Universal Substance" (Spinoza), a "Creative Force" (Coffin). The Bible uses several terms for God. The Hebrew term generally translated God (Genesis 1:1) is Elohim. It probably means the Mighty One and is always used to designate the Creator God.

The shorter form of Elohim, El, is used often in combination with other words to reveal elements in the nature of God: El-Elyon, God most high (Genesis 14:18), El Shaddai, Almighty God or the God of Sufficiency (Genesis 17:1), El Roi, the God who sees (Genesis 16:13).

Yahweh or Jehovah (*American Standard Version*) appears rarely in the King James Version. The Hebrews considered this personal name of God too holy to pronounce. The King James translators respected this and usually substituted LORD in its place. This term too appears in combinations such as Jehovah-jireh, the Lord who provided (Genesis 22:13), Jehovah-Rapha, the Lord who heals (Exodus 15:26), or Jehovah-Nissi, the Lord is our banner (Exodus 17:8-15).

Each of these names simply gives further insight into the character of God. Each act of God in history revealed some new aspects of His being. Taken together they reveal the Being we call God. One definition of God is "an eternal personal Being of absolute knowledge, power, and goodness."

II. THE NATURE OF GOD
(Deuteronomy 4:14-23)

This passage of Scripture does deal with the nature or essence of God. The children of Israel had dwelt in the midst of idolatry. They had seen nations around them who worshiped idols or gods fashioned from material objects. God's Word to them through Moses emphasized that the God which they served was not one that could be grasped through a physical sense: " . . . Ye saw no manner of similitude on the day that the LORD spake unto you in Horeb out of the midst of the fire." They heard God but they did not see a material form that could be imitated.

Although God is spirit and could have assumed some form that could be sensed, He did not choose to do so "Lest ye corrupt yourselves, and make you a graven image" (Deuteronomy 4:16). It was for this very reason that God had given one of the Ten Commandments. God was not like any earthly object, therefore He said, "Thou shalt not make unto thee any graven image, or any likeness or any thing that is in heaven above, or that is in the earth beneath, or that is in the water under the earth" (Exodus 20:4).

On this discourse by Moses he spelled out even more broadly the fact that they were not to conceive of God in any material form, and then he broadened the area of prohibition so that they would recognize that every area was forbidden. Included were things "on the earth" (verse 17), "in the air" (verse 17), in "the waters" (verse 18), or in "heaven" (verse 19). There was no reason for the Hebrews to miss the meaning of God. His being was of such a nature that it could not be copied by man. In this passage the command is further emphasized by its repetition and extra warning in verse 23: "Take heed unto yourselves, lest ye forget the covenant of the LORD your God, which he made with you, and make you a graven image, or the likeness of any thing, which the LORD thy God hath forbidden thee." Even the covenant was bound up with the prohibition against making images.

SPIRITUALITY

What then is the nature of God? Spirituality is the basic element in the nature of God. Jesus mentioned this in His discourse with the Samaritan woman (John 4:21-24). He said, "God is a Spirit." Probably this should be translated: "God is Spirit." This distinguishes Him from anything related to the material.

Several things are involved in Spirit: (1) God is invisible. Paul mentioned "the image of the invisible God" (Colossians 1:15) and "the King eternal, . . . invisible" (1 Timothy 1:17). All material objects are of a visible nature. Spirit is not. (2) God is incorporeal (not confined to a material body). Jesus said, "A spirit hath not flesh and bones" (Luke 24:39). God does not have bodily parts and passions such as man. Man is limited because of this, but God is unlimited. This fact about God is why the prohibitions of making graven images were so strong. Because God is invisible and without a material body, He cannot be seen by physical senses, but is known by the soul in the spirit of man.

Of course, the Bible uses anthropomorphic expressions (giving human characteristics) of God mentioning His hands, feet, arms, eyes, and ears. He is said to see, feel, hear, and walk. These terms are only used to make God understandable to man. The unlimited God has to be brought by these means into the comprehension of limited men.

Another fact to be noted is that God can, when He chooses, be made manifest in visible form. The "Spirit descending from heaven like a dove" (John 1:32), and the Angel of the Lord in the Old Testament (Genesis 16:7, 10, 13; 22:11) are both examples of this fact. It was something of this nature that the elders of Israel beheld when the Word says that they "saw the God of Israel." All these must be interpreted in the light of John 1:18 which says, "No man hath seen God at any time."

Some argue that God must have a body since man is made in the image and likeness of God. But this does not refer to the body of man. Man has intellect, will, emotions, and a moral nature. It is in the realm of these that he bears a likeness to God. All of these are invisible qualities. The "new man . . . created in righteousness and true holiness" (Ephesians 4:24) is an example of these qualities.

PERSONALITY

Many of the non-Christian world views of God do not admit personality as a part of the nature of God. Pantheism sees no personality in God—only an unconscious force working in the world. Polytheism recognizes idols and idols have no personality. True religion is communion between two persons—God and man. True religion would not be possible without personality in God.

The *Free Will Baptist Treatise* describes God as the true and living God. Idol gods are dead and lifeless. They cannot walk, speak, hear, or see. Paul called them "these vanities" (Acts 14:15). Paul commended the Thessalonians because they had "turned . . . from idols to serve the living and true God" (1 Thessalonians 1:9).

When we think of personality, we think of intelligence, will, self-consciousness, individuality, and even emotion. The names given to God in the Bible denote personality: the Lord will provide (Genesis 22:13, 14), the Lord is my shepherd (Psalm 23:1), the Lord is present (Ezekiel 48:35). Personal pronouns are used of God in a way that could only denote personality (John 17:2).

That God repents (Genesis 6:6), grieves (6:6), is angry (1 Kings 11:9), is jealous (Deuteronomy 6:15), loves (Revelation 3:19), and hates (Proverbs 6:16) are attributes of personality. Such could not mark an ultimate force or some other impersonal god. Even His works demonstrate personality. He created the universe and man (Genesis 1:1, 26). He continues to sustain it and maintain His creation in existence (Colossians 1:15-17; Hebrews 1:3).

It is in Jesus that the climax of the revelation of the personality of God comes. He revealed God as a Father who cares for His children. The hairs of their head are numbered. Not a sparrow falls but God notes it, and His consciousness of His children is much

23

greater than this. They have but to ask Him and He supplies their needs as they ask in faith believing.

UNITY OF GOD

A discussion of the nature of God would be incomplete without a mention of the unity of God. If we are not careful in our teaching, we will leave the impression that there are three Gods: the Father, the Son, and the Holy Spirit. The Bible, however, portrays a unity in the Godhead throughout: "Hear, O Israel: The LORD our God is one LORD" (Deuteronomy 6:4). To believe in three Gods is Tritheism. This is similar to polytheism, the belief in many gods.

The idea of the unity of God does not rule out our belief of a plurality of persons in the Godhead which is referred to as the Trinity. However, caution should be used in the employment of the idea of a person. It is not to be used in the sense of separate, distinct individuals or persons as we generally use it. This would lead to Tritheism.

Since the doctrine of the Trinity is a revelation that has nothing with which to be compared in earthly things, it is difficult for the human mind to conceive. Here are facts that must be stressed, however, in any teaching of the doctrine: (1) In both the Old and New Testaments, God is revealed as one. (2) This unity is fundamental, but the Bible also reveals that God is more than unity. There was a diversity of manifestations of God. (3) In the New Testament, and intimated in the Old, this diversity becomes a Trinity. (4) The work of Father, Son, and Holy Spirit are all the work of God. (5) The work of each is inclusive of the other. (6) It is the Second Person, the Son, who always manifests God to man.

We must always be careful not to try to simplify God. God is a Supreme Being, unlimited where we are limited. Anytime we try to explain Him in human terms, we oversimplify and make Him less than what He is. As our *Treatise* says: "Finite beings cannot comprehend Him." We must learn all we can about Him, but then remember that He is multiplied times greater than anything we can discover—How Great Thou Art!

III. THE ATTRIBUTES OF GOD
(Romans 1)

In discussing the nature of God, the main emphasis was on the essence or substance of God's being. The attributes of God are an analysis of His being or a closer description of His nature and being. The attributes are particular ways in which God exists and operates. They make known to man more objectively the way God is and acts.

The attributes of God have been divided into various categories by different writers. Most divide them into two categories but different names are given to these categories by the writers. Probably the most used categories are the natural and moral or the moral and non-moral. As in *Faith For Today*, this writer will use the natural and moral categories.

The natural attributes of God are those which do not convey the idea of moral character. Listed in our *Treatise* these are "self-existent, eternal, immutable, omnipresent, omniscient, omnipotent, independent." The moral attributes, of course, are those which convey the thought of moral character. Those listed in the *Treatise* depict God as "good, wise, holy, just, and merciful." Note the following about each of these attributes.

SELF-EXISTENCE

Man is dependent upon God for his existence; therefore, he is a dependent creature. God, however, is dependent solely upon Himself. As Jesus said, "The Father hath life in himself" (John 5:26).

The ground of His existence is in Himself and is affected by no outside source.

Even the existence of the universe may be compared to God's existence. The universe, though great it is, is dependent upon God for sustenance (Colossians 1:17). Thomas Aquinas, the great Catholic theologian, said that He is "the first cause, Himself uncaused." God is living (1 Timothy 3:15) and is the source of all that lives.

ETERNITY

God goes beyond all the limitations of time. When a believer comes into possession of eternal life, this only extends into the eternity yet to come. God's eternity stretches into the eternity that was before time began. The psalmist well expressed this thought when he wrote: "Before the mountains were brought forth, or ever thou hadst formed the earth and the world, even from everlasting to everlasting, thou art God" (Psalm 90:2).

Time, as man knows it, is surely real to God for He made it. But while God knows of time and recognizes it, He is not limited by it as man is. He existed before time began and will continue to exist when time is declared to be no more (Hebrews 1:10-12).

God is free from all succession of time for He made time. As one writer described this attribute of timelessness in God, "It is duration, without beginning or end; existence without bounds or dimension; present without past or future. His eternity is youth, without infancy or old age; life, without birth or death; today, without yesterday or tomorrow."

IMMUTABILITY

The attribute of immutability in God is often misunderstood. It should be recognized that this attribute is used in relation to the character of God and not in regard to His dealings with men.

When the Bible speaks of God repenting (Genesis 6:6; Jonah 3:10), this does not involve any change in the character and purposes of God. God did not change His attitude toward the Ninevites, but the Ninevites themselves changed. When they changed from ungodliness to godliness and from disobedience to obedience, His attitude did change but not His character. The change was in accord with the principles of His character.

Thus by immutability we refer to the fact that God's nature is unchangeable. In Malachi 3:6 He said, "I am the LORD, I change not." James wrote to us about "the Father of lights, with whom is no variableness, neither shadow of turning" (James 1:17). This character of unchangeableness is the basis for the faithfulness of God. All the words of God can be trusted for He shall not change. There is some evidence that the statement, "I AM THAT I AM" (Exodus 3:14), should be translated, "I shall always be what I have been." The very perfection of His nature would rule out any change.

OMNIPRESENCE

By the omnipresence of God we mean that God is everywhere present at all times. This does not mean that He is present in a bodily sense. This is a spiritual presence and not a material one. In Jeremiah 23:23, 24 God asked, "Am I a God at hand, . . . and not a God afar off? Can any hide himself in secret places that I shall not see him? . . . Do not I fill heaven and earth?" And the psalmist wrote:

"Whither shall I go from thy spirit? or whither shall I flee from thy presence?" (139:7—use also verses 8-12).

OMNISCIENCE

God knows all things. His knowledge of all things is perfect in every sense. It is absolutely comprehensive as Solomon wrote: "The eyes of the LORD are in every place, beholding the evil and the good" (Proverbs 15:3). This perfect knowledge covers all that is in nature. He even knows "the number of the stars; he calleth them all by their names" (Psalm 147:4). This knowledge reaches to small details, for a sparrow "shall not fall to the ground without your Father" (Matthew 10:29). Nor is His knowledge limited by time. He knows the past (Acts 15:18), present (Proverbs 5:21), and future (Isaiah 48:5-8; 49:9, 10).

OMNIPOTENCE AND INDEPENDENCE

God's power is of such an unlimited nature that He can bring to pass what He wills. Job said, "I know that thou canst do every thing" (42:2). All power in the universe whether it be physical or spiritual has its source in God. There is no bounds nor limitation to His power, and even Satan is subject to it.

Because God is omnipotent, omniscient, and self-existent, He has no need to be dependent upon any existing thing. All creation exists because of God, but He existed before His creation and He is not dependent upon it for His continued existence.

GOODNESS

All the qualities of God which answer to man's conception of an ideal person are included in the goodness of God. God is good and all good is related to Him (Mark 10:18). Good has no existence outside of God. This goodness of God includes His love, benevolence, mercy, and grace. He is spoken of in the Bible as "the God of love" (2 Corinthians 13:11), as benevolent toward His creation (Psalm 147:9, 15, 16), as "rich in mercy" (Ephesians 2:4), and as rich in grace (Ephesians 1:7).

WISDOM

"Wisdom is the intelligence of God displayed in the choice of the highest ends and of the fittest means for the accomplishment of those ends" (Thiessen) God alone possesses this fullness of wisdom (Romans 16:27). This wisdom of God is especially displayed in attaining His own glory.

HOLINESS

God is absolute in His holiness. The holiness of man is relative. It is limited by man's past. God is separate from all that defiles and His being is void of all evil. God's character always conforms to what is true, faithful, and righteous. He is called "the Holy One of Israel" over thirty times in Isaiah. "The LORD our God is holy," wrote the psalmist (99:9, compare Job 34:10, Isaiah 57:15).

JUSTICE AND MERCY

Included in the holiness of God is the element of severity toward sin, or justice. This causes God to impose righteous laws upon man and to execute penalties upon the breaches of those laws. This justice of God involves His scorn of sin, but related to it is the mercy of God. This is that quality of His goodness which leads Him to seek the temporal and spiritual welfare of sinners. When man is in misery and distress because of his transgressions, God comes to his aid (Ephesians 2:4, 5).

All of these doctrines should be studied with Bible in hand recognizing that the Word of God contains all that has been revealed about the character of God. Inferences may be drawn from nature and conscience, but it is in the Word of God that the truth about the character of God may be known.

Remember always that Jesus Christ, the Son of God, is the greatest revelation of God. What can be seen to be true in Christ is true of the character of God. The love of God is the chief quality portrayed, yet His severity toward sin may be seen in the death of Christ. The thoughts of men cannot compare to what is revealed in Christ.

Chapter Two

3

The Incarnation of Christ

BACKGROUND

Perhaps no other doctrine has been attacked more viciously than the doctrine of the Virgin Birth, which is closely interwoven with the incarnation. It would probably be safe to say that no doctrine has been understood as vaguely as the doctrine of the incarnation. How could God the Son take upon Himself the form of sinful flesh, come to die for sinful man, yet remain divine?

The Bible seems to anticipate no difficulty in the doctrine. Like all the rest of God's Word, if it is accepted by faith, the difficulty vanishes.

It is remarkable how the New Testament writers agree on the subject of Christ's divinity. That is, it is remarkable from the human standpoint. If the inspiration of the Bible is accepted, there is nothing remarkable about it, for surely one should expect the Holy Spirit to agree with Himself.

But because there are many even in the ranks of Christianity who do not accept the truth of the incarnation, it is necessary that those who do accept it be able to discuss the subject with some degree of clarity.

God was definitely in Christ reconciling the world unto Himself.

OUTLINE

I. **Incarnation Defined**
   A. **The Word Made Flesh (John 1:1-5, 14)**
   B. **The Likeness of Men (Philippians 2:5-11)**
II. **Incarnation Defended**
   A. **Identification in Suffering (Hebrews 2:9, 10)**
   B. **Identification in the Flesh (Hebrews 2:11-13)**
   C. **Identification in Death (Hebrews 2:14-18)**

INTRODUCTION

Let us look to Erich Sauer for an introduction to the doctrine of the incarnation. He wrote: "And then the incomprehensible came to pass. The Son forsook the splendour of heaven and became really as a man as ourselves. Surrendering the eternal form of God above all worlds He voluntarily entered into human relationships within the world. Leaving the free, unconditioned, world-ruling absoluteness of the Divine form, the Son entered the limits of time and space of the creature. The eternal Word became a human soul and emptied Himself of His world-embracing power as Ruler. The self-seeking may hold with tenacity even strange and unjustly acquired possessions, as being welcome 'prey' (Philippians 2:6); but He, the primary fount of love, did not regard even His own original and legitimate possession, the Divine form and Divine position, as something to be maintained at all costs, but surrendered in order to save us. He descended 'into the lower regions of the earth' (Ephesians 4:9), so as to take us, the redeemed, with and in Himself up to the heights of heaven. God became man that man might become godly. He became poor for our sakes that we through His poverty might become rich (2 Corinthians 8:9)."

Thus the incarnation is the central point in our salvation and in reality, the center of history. All history revolves around that point in time when God became man.

I. INCARNATION DEFINED

A. The Word Made Flesh
(John 1:1-5, 14)

John is almost formal in his presentation of "the Word" who was made flesh. These first five verses of the first chapter of John give us insights into who the Word was and what He was like that are not found elsewhere. Notice these basic facts about the Word:

1. The Word was from eternity (verses 1, 2).

2. The Word was with God in His activities (verse 1).

3. The Word was divine (verse 1).

4. The Word was so related to Creation that nothing came into existence except through His power (verse 3).

5. The Word was the source of life and imparted this to man (verse 4).

6. The Word was the source and means of the revelation of God to men (verse 5).

John introduces us to "The Word" without any explanation. This term is usually used simply of word or speech. It is used by John of the acting reality of the person of God. It is not a figure of speech but the Person, the pre-existing Son of God, who came as Jesus Christ in the form of man. It was *He who manifested* God in a way which He had not been manifested in the Law or the Prophets. This Scripture tells us about Christ before the incarnation.

John describes the eternal pre-existence of the Word in several ways: (1) He was in the beginning. (2) He was with God. (3) He was

God (divine). (4) He was the Creator of all things. (5) He was the source of life. (6) He was the source of light. That He was "in the beginning" describes a state which existed and implies that He was without beginning Himself. This existence of His was an enduring and unlimited state of being.

Probably that He "was with God" and "the Word was God" are a distinct repetition of the same thought; although John is maintaining the distinction within the Godhead. The Word was with God but the first and second persons must be distinguished; however, the Word was distinctly of the essence of God. In fact, He was the very God.

Verse 2 is recorded to make sure the reader catches the distinction between the two persons of the Godhead. Actually, this verse is a repetition of the first two clauses of verse 1 and adds no new thought. John combines the two thoughts to bring the reader to his statement in verse 3.

"All things were made by him" is speaking of the whole world. One writer has well observed that the Scriptures never explicitly say, "Christ made the world," but implies that the Father made the world through the Son. The Son never works of Himself but as the revelation of the Father. Paul mentions "the Father, of whom are all things, . . . and one Lord Jesus Christ, by whom are all things" (1 Corinthians 8:6). Elsewhere he says, "by him were all things created" (Colossians 1:16). Both passages use "by" in the instrumental sense.

In verse 3 John is also stressing two other facts: the pre-existence of Christ the Word and the creation of matter. Some men argue for the eternal nature of matter. The Gnostics (a mystical religion combining philosophy and Christianity) held to this view and believed that it was uncreated. The beginning of gnosticism (pronounced "nas-te-sizm") may have been in existence in John's day. He definitely refutes such a view and demonstrates that matter was created, and nothing came into being except through the divine Word.

When John says that "life" was in Him, he was not just referring to spiritual life nor the recovery of blessedness lost through sin. The Word was the source of all life to the creatures of the universe. Truly He is the source of recovered spiritual life, but it must be recognized that He mediates all life to created beings.

A particular view of this life is that "the life was the light of men." Light is a condition of life in the material world. Without light all life would soon degenerate and die. This is true also in the spiritual world. The condition of all development and furtherance of life is in light. The Word is the source of this light. This does not mean just the teaching of Jesus but refers to the enlightening and life-sustaining influence of the eternal Son of God. All knowledge, all purity, all love, all happiness result from the light of which He is the source. Verse 9 says: "That was the true Light, which lighteth every man that cometh into the world." Recognizing that "God is light," John elsewhere wrote, "If we walk in the light, as he is in the light, we have fellowship one with another, and the blood of Jesus Christ his Son cleanseth us from all sin" (1 John 1:7).

The world lies in wickedness (1 John 5:19). Satan is the ruler of the kingdom of darkness. It was into this darkness that "the light shineth" (John 1:5). Although the light shining probably refers to the total process of the Eternal Word shining in the darkness of the world, both by the Old Testament and New Testament revelations, in a special sense it is referring to the coming of the Incarnate Word in the person of Jesus Christ. Every aspect of revelation, including every scattered fragment gleaned in the Old Testament, was important, but it was in Jesus that "the true Light" (John 1:9) was made clear. The incarnation was the climax of the shining of that Light from Heaven.

John's sad commentary is that "the darkness comprehended it not" (verse 5). The Incarnate Word appeared and even His chosen people did not recognize Him, for "He came unto his own, and his own received him not" (John 1:11). The "darkness," of course, refers to the total amount of the world's rejection of revelation. The darkness of the world just could not understand the light from Heaven since it contrasted so much with the darkness. Darkness and light force out each other.

John's climax to these verses comes in 1:14. This pre-existent Word of God, which was the Light of the world, came into the world. In this verse he explains the manner of His appearance: "And the Word was made flesh, and dwelt among us, (and we beheld his glory, the glory as of the only begotten of the Father,) full of grace and truth." When it says that He "was made flesh," it means that He became a man or took upon Himself human nature.

It is from this statement and others like it that the concept of incarnation is derived. The word *incarnate* means "in the flesh." The term is used to describe what takes place when "one of a higher order than man, and of a different nature, assumes the appearance of man, or becomes a man." In this instance the second person of the Trinity, the Word, became a man identified as Jesus of Nazareth. He was truly God but through the incarnation became truly man as well.

That "the Word was made flesh" implies a change of state. Every man is in the flesh, but the word *incarnation* would not be used of his state for he has not previously existed. But He who made all things and had prior and eternal existence only as Spirit now entered into time as a man and "dwelt among us." The Word lived temporarily among men as one of them. In all appearances He was a man. He ate, drank, slept, and was seen of man for over thirty years. During this period He was hungry, tired, and even tempted. In every way, except sin, He identified with the race of man.

John is careful that He is not identified only as a man, however. While He was on earth and in the flesh, "we beheld his glory, the glory as of the only begotten of the Father." The majesty, dignity, and splendor of the Word was that which was appropriate to the Son of God. His rank and character were expressed by His works and through special events in His life. John had shared with the other inner circle disciples that outstanding expression of His glory and majesty in the transfiguration on the mountain.

As the Word was made flesh, He was "full of grace and truth." He was full of signs of goodness. As the "only begotten of the Father," He sustained a peculiar relation to the Father not possible to any of the other sons of God.

The *Free Will Baptist Treatise* describes the incarnation thusly: "The Word, which in the beginning was with God and which was God, by whom all things were made, condescended to a state of humiliation in being united with human nature and becoming like us, pollution and sin excepted. In this state, as a subject of the law, He was liable to the infirmities of our nature, was tempted as we are, but lived our example, perfect obedience to the divine requirements. As Christ was made of the seed of David, according to the flesh, He is "the Son of man," and as the divine existence is the fountain from which He proceeded, and was the only agency by which He was begotten, He is "the Son of God," being the only begotten of the Father, and the only incarnation of the Divine Being."

B. The Likeness of Men (Philippians 2:5-11)

Paul develops the truth of the incarnation in this passage. His emphasis is on the likeness of the Word to the fleshly nature which He assumed when He "became flesh and dwelt among us." The passage develops out of Paul's exhortation to the Philippians to assume humility. By giving this reference to the incarnation, he sets forth the example of Christ to enforce the duty of humility upon believers. The self-denial of Christ enforces the duty upon each believer to act always in an attitude of self-giving.

"Let this mind be in you," Paul said, and then interpreted which one: "which was also in Christ Jesus" (verse 5). The mind or attitude referred to is that self-denying attitude of Christ which allowed Him to become incarnate, to take upon Himself our humanity. But it also included His further humiliation in that He suffered the most extreme suffering while in the flesh, even to the point of a degrading death.

Verse 6 explains the first thought mentioned here: "Who, being in the form of God, thought it not robbery to be equal with God." This former phrase explains the status of Christ in His pre-incarnate situation. He was in the "form of God." This expresses His divinity. This does not include only the nature of God but as the writer of Hebrews described Him, "the brightness of his glory, and the express image of his person" (Hebrews 1:3).

A further proof that His divinity is emphasized here is found in the phrase which says that He "thought it not robbery to be equal with God." No one can misunderstand this concept that He was "equal with God." Alford translated this phrase in this manner: "deemed not his equality with God a matter for grasping." Someone else has translated it that "his equality with God was not a thing to be attained." The divinity of Christ was a condition from eternity. He did not become God, but had always been God. He was divine and did not have to attain such a status.

Although Christ was divine, His incarnation demanded that He appear to man in a different nature than that of God. So He did not further Himself but rather "made himself of no reputation" (verse 7). Rather than using His divine powers as an opportunity for self-exaltation, He used them for His self-abasement. This phrase can be translated, "he emptied himself." It has been generally interpreted to mean that, while in His incarnate form, He laid aside the independent exercise of His relative attributes. He ceased during this state to reflect the glory which He had with the Father in the heavenlies (John 17:5) but resumed it at His glorification.

The method by which He "emptied himself" was taking "upon him the form of a servant." This stands in great contrast to the previous verse but gives us an exact picture of the incarnation. He who was "equal with God" emptied Himself and took on the "form of a servant."

This condition as a servant is further described in the following phrase: "and was made in the likeness of men." He was not just a man but this "likeness of men" must be interpreted that the Son of God was manifest in the flesh and nature of man. The form of humanity was the device by which He revealed Himself to men.

Verse 8 relates further acts of that self-humiliation through the incarnation. Being found in this human appearance, Paul tells us that "he humbled himself, and became obedient unto death." This describes the extent of the humiliation of Christ. His becoming subject to death in the incarnate condition is also the climax of His humiliation. The incarnation would have been without meaning had He not gone to this ultimate extent. In fact, the very purpose of His coming was "the death of the cross." His life in the flesh had no meaning except as it climaxed in that death. His death would have had no meaning for man had He not come in "the form of a servant" and "in fashion as a man."

But the consequences of the humiliation of Christ was His exaltation. This exaltation is related in the following verses. He who emptied Himself of that prior glory which He had with the Father, "God also hath highly exalted him" (verse 9). The humiliation involved the Son's becoming incarnate. The exaltation surely included the resurrection of Christ and His ascension back to the Father and His taking His position at the right hand of the Father. Because He rendered voluntary and perfect obedience to the Father, He gave Him "a name which is above every name." The Father, in one sense, was greater than the incarnate Son (John

14:28). It was to the incarnate Son that the exaltation came. Jesus was exalted from this lowly state to the throne in Heaven.

The "name which is above every name" has been interpreted in many ways. Some writers have even changed it to mean the "glory" given to Jesus. It would appear though that Paul is referring to the very name Jesus, which was the name borne by the Son of God in His humiliation. It is this name which He continues to bear in His exaltation.

Verse 10 would seem to bear this out for it is "at the name of Jesus" that "every knee should bow." It is the intent of the exaltation of Jesus from the humiliation of the incarnation to bring Him to this reception of praise and honor. Universal prayer is to be offered in the name of Jesus. Prayer to the Father is to be made in that exalted name. "Calling upon the name of the Lord" became synonymous with prayer (Romans 10:13; 1 Corinthians 1:2).

This exaltation would be among angels, "things in heaven," men, "things in earth," and even the dead, "things under the earth." His exaltation would be by universal acclaim for "every tongue should confess that Jesus Christ is Lord" (verse 11). Just as everyone approaching God would do so by "calling upon the name of the Lord," those calling upon Him would go forth confessing Him as Lord. They would recognize His divinity and profess Him to be worthy of worship. The end of all Christ's mediatorial work, of course, would be "the glory of God the Father." The issue of all confession of Christ brings glory to God for that was the purpose of the work of Christ.

II. INCARNATION DEFENDED

A. Identification in Suffering
(Hebrews 2:9, 10)

The writer of the book of Hebrews sought to show that salvation in Jesus Christ was better than anything that was presented in the Old Testament Scriptures. The revelation in Christ was fuller than any previous revelation (Hebrews 1:1, 2). He was better than angels because of His position (1:4-14). But one of the chief advantages of Jesus was in His identification with man through the incarnation.

Through the incarnation, He who was to God "the express image of his person" (1:3) came into a position "a little lower than the angels" (2:9). The purpose of the incarnation was "for the suffering of death." His sufferings were necessary for Him to become our Redeemer. This was accomplished when He tasted death for every man. That He was crowned with glory and honour" is a reference to His exaltation after His suffering, which was discussed in the previous section.

There are those who found such suffering as that endured by Christ as unbecoming to a member of the Godhead. Verse 10 is an assurance that His extreme humiliation in His sufferings was not unsuitable or unworthy of the second person of the Trinity. Rather, it was altogether in correspondence with His being and worthy of His wisdom and love. "It became him" in that it was the most suitable way for Him to attain the will and purpose of God.

The Jews felt a strong offense to the cross. It did not suit their ideas of the glory and kingly triumph of the Messiah. These Jewish Christians to whom the author of Hebrews directed his message may have compared the humiliation of Christ in His sufferings to the Jewish concept. But the writer of Hebrews wanted them to get a full idea about Christ. Truly He was humiliated in the incarnation and in the sufferings which so identified Him with man, but it was also important to realize that the resurrection and exaltation of Christ gave promise of the future glory He would share with those who trusted in Him.

The way of suffering and the cross was worthy of God's high purpose. He "for whom are all things, and by whom are all things" planned to bring "many sons unto glory" through the means of the incarnation.

The perfection of the "captain of their salvation" refers to the accomplishment or making complete of the glory of Christ. The glory of Christ or His exaltation came after He had effected a means for the salvation of man. The proposed or destined end was the glory of Christ in all this.

B. Identification in the Flesh
   (Hebrews 2:11-13)

The words *sanctify* and *make holy* are the same in the Greek. Our word for sanctuary refers to a place made holy. Saints are people who are made holy. The word refers to the selecting out and adopting for God's service. Often inherent holiness is emphasized rather than the idea of setting apart for the use of God. Actually the believer's sanctification or holiness is the glory of God being accomplished in a believer. It is not finished yet in the sense that the believer may claim a natural inborn holiness such as God has.

Verse 11 tells us that the one who sets apart for the use of God and the one who is thus dedicated to the work of God are all "of one." Christ is of God and God is the source of our sanctification. Both are of the same divine stock and have the same heavenly Father. Christ, though divine, was in no way ashamed of the incarnation which identified Him with man: "He is not ashamed to call them brethren." He could not be ashamed for His relation to man was just a means by which He was to accomplish His glory and all of the things which happened to Him originated in the plan and purpose of God.

To support this argument the writer quotes Psalm 22:22. This verse stands in the prophetic psalm between the sufferings and the triumphant portion of the psalm. The concept seems to be that He who was identified in the flesh with men, even to the point of extreme sufferings, was willing likewise to be identified with them in His exaltation. He was made "perfect" and now "in the midst of the church" He is still willing to acknowledge them as brethren. Notice how that the Lord did refer to the disciples as brethren after the Resurrection (Matthew 28:10; John 20:17).

The exact reference of the phrase, "I will put my trust in him," is difficult to pinpoint. It may be a reference to Psalm 18:2 or Isaiah 12:2. The second quote in verse 13 is probably from Isaiah 8:18. There the prophet rebukes King Ahaz for his lack of trust in the Lord and for turning to the Assyrians for help in the time of crisis. These words may be predictive of the Messiah and His disciples in a later situation. Just as Judah and the people had a hope for future deliverance from the suffering in that day, so there was a glorification to come to the Son of God after He was identified in the flesh and through His sufferings with mankind. It is such a blessed thought to man to know that his Savior was identified with him.

C. Identification in Death
(Hebrews 2:14-18)

Christ was identified with man in that He was born through a woman. In His sharing our humanity and living His life like us, He was further identified with us. He hungered, thirsted, was tired and sleepy just as any man. He was truly human in that He shared "flesh and blood" with mankind. However, this sharing of the humanity of man was just a device by which He could become identified in death with man. God had set death as the penalty for sin. Since all men had sinned, the death penalty rested upon all men and had to be paid. Jesus became incarnate that He might die and pay the penalty for man's sin. By releasing man from the death penalty, He released him from the power of Satan and brought him into a renewed relation to God.

Death had always ruled in the realm of the human. Genesis 5 is a commentary on God's statement to Adam and Eve that if they broke His commandment they would die. Every man's epitaph (with the exception of Enoch) is there written, "and he died." This fear of death kept man in fear and subject to the bondage of that fear. But the coming of Christ broke both: (1) It freed man from the fear of death. (2) It broke the shackles of sin which held man in bondage to sin. Man's nature was prone to sin, but through the redemption made possible by the death of Christ man can now yield himself to God and the development of holiness.

Until Christ came, death was always looked upon as bad. It was the penalty for sin. But Christ conquered death and removed its sting. The agency of Satan in death was removed. Now we may view death as merely a channel through which we pass from this life into eternal existence with Christ. Just as death was a passage for Jesus from humiliation to the new and glorious exaltation, so it is to the believer a passageway into a life of triumph and blessedness. Of course, to the unbeliever who does not unite himself by faith to Christ, it remains a terror for it is punishment for sins.

Jesus did not identify Himself with the angels. They are not subject to death (verse 16). Rather "he took on him the seed of Abraham," for this was a race subject to death. The phrase, "seed of Abraham," probably refers also to His special identification with the Jewish race, which had especially been chosen as a vehicle for revelation: "He came unto his own, and his own received him not" (John 1:11).

Verse 17 shows how it was necessary for Him to become incarnate and fully identified with man to accomplish His mediatorial work. Real humanity with its sufferings, temptations, and sympathies were involved for He was fully made "like unto his brethren." It was necessary that the high priest who mediated for man should be taken from among man. An angel could not die for man. Had God simply, by His own power, pronounced man free from his guilt, He would not have been a just God: "It behoved him to be made like unto his brethren . . . to make reconciliation for the sins of the people."

Actually, it should be recognized that the high priestly work of Christ is carried on in the heavenlies (5:5-10; 6:19, 20). His incarnation, suffering and death, the identification with us, were all prerequisites to His becoming our High Priest. Not His death but His presentation of the sacrifice in the Holy Place accomplished the atonement for our sins.

His identification with us is emphasized in verse 18. It is through the power of sympathy, acquired through His becoming man, that we especially feel His help. Surely the incarnation gave Him no new power but to man there is a special meaning in His becoming one of us. That He did what He did for us makes salvation even more meaningful to us. And with this the knowledge that the God-man is now interceding for us as our High Priest gives us encouragement as we approach the throne of the Almighty God.

Chapter Three

4

The Atonement and Mediation of Christ

BACKGROUND

Since the subject of the atonement and mediation of Christ is so vital to one's right relationship with God, it is good to be thoroughly grounded in the truth of these great doctrines.

All Bible students are familiar with the expressions of the blood of Christ and its power to cleanse from sin. "Without [the] shedding of blood, [there] is no remission."

One needs to be careful, however, of making this cleansing from sin a mechanical thing. There is vastly more involved than a mere washing such as the washing of an article of clothing. The cleansing of the soul by the blood of Christ is a dynamic act vitally related to the life of Christ for "the life is in the blood."

Surely, no one would say that the Holy Spirit literally takes the soul out of the body, washes it in the blood of the Lamb, and replaces the soul into the body. But something just as real and more dynamic happens, and the blood of Jesus Christ does cleanse from all sins.

Such statements regarding the blood are used in the Scriptures to convey as nearly as possible what happens when an individual trusts Christ as Savior and Lord. If there had been a better way to express it, God would have used it. But it should be remembered that there is more than mechanical cleansing involved. There is a complete recreation and a removal of all the guilt and stain of sin.

The subject should be approached reverently and with a desire to learn as much as possible, but one needs to realize that it can never be fully understood by finite minds.

OUTLINE

I. The Shed Blood of Christ (Hebrews 9:15-26)
II. The Vicarious Sufferings of Christ (Hebrews 9:1-14)
III. The Victorious Accomplishment of Christ (Hebrews 8:1-13; 9:27, 28)
IV. The Intercessory Work of Christ (Hebrews 7:25, 28)

INTRODUCTION

This exposition like many others in this doctrinal series will not be of a particular passage of the Scriptures but of the particular doctrine to which it is devoted. These passages in Hebrews which are setting forth the general idea of the atonement and mediation of Christ will serve only as background Scriptures for the study.

The atonement is vitally linked with the death of Christ. In many instances the two are mentioned or discussed as the same. At times the death of Christ or His atonement for man's sins is referred to as the "work of Christ." The total work of Christ would involve His acts in soul-winning, His many deeds which were beneficial to man, His ministry of preaching and teaching, and many other things. But all fall into insignificance in the face of His death for our atonement. This "work" of Christ was a work because it resulted from a definite choice on His part to so benefit man.

I. THE SHED BLOOD OF CHRIST
(Hebrews 9:15-26)

This century has seen the rise of the teaching which makes light of the "blood theology." Those who still teach that man is redeemed by the blood of the Lamb are said to hold to a "slaughter-house" religion. The modern strains of Christianity have sought to prove that the shed blood of Christ was not an essential element in the contribution of Christ to man's salvation. But the importance of the death and shed blood of Christ is found in the fact that His teachings and all New Testament teachings lose their significance without it.

1. The Old Testament Scriptures foretold the shedding of the blood of Christ for man's sins. Both by type and prophecy is this revealed. Many would trace it in type from the shed blood of the animal slain to provide clothing to cover the nakedness of Adam and Eve (Genesis 3:21). Sacrifice, costing the shed blood of the victim, may be traced from the sacrifice of Abel (Genesis 4:4), the substitute offering for Isaac (Genesis 22:13), the Passover Lamb prior to the exodus from Egypt (Exodus 12:1-28), and many other Old Testament offerings. His death is foretold in many prophecies (Isaiah 53: 4-6; Psalm 22).

2. The death of Christ is important enough to be mentioned directly over 175 times in the New Testament. Its prominence in the New Testament is stressed by several facts: (a) It is the chief purpose of the incarnation. Jesus Himself said, "For even the Son of man came not to be ministered unto, but to minister, and to give his life a ransom for many" (Mark 10:45). The writer of Hebrews wrote about Jesus "who was made a little lower than the angels for the suffering of death, crowned with glory and honour; that he by

the grace of God should taste death for every man" (2:9). If Jesus was "manifested to take away our sins" (1 John 3:5), we must search for that element of His incarnation which dealt with our sins. Paul tells us that He was "set forth to be a propitiation through faith in his blood" (Romans 3:25). So He came not primarily to teach, set an example, or preach, but to die and shed His blood for our sins.

(b) His death and the shedding of His blood is the basic theme of the gospel. His death is a vital item in Paul's summation of the gospel (1 Corinthians 15:1-4). John writes that "the blood of Jesus Christ his Son cleanseth us from all sin" (1 John 1:7). Paul said that we were "made nigh by the blood of Christ" (Ephesians 2:13). And Peter, giving a summary of the gospel message, declared: "Forasmuch as ye know that ye were not redeemed with corruptible things, as silver and gold, from your vain conversation received by tradition from your fathers; But with the precious blood of Christ, as of a lamb without blemish and without spot" (1 Peter 1:18, 19).

3. The doctrine of the shed blood of Christ is essential to Christianity. It is not a religion based primarily upon the teachings of a man. It stands or falls upon the importance of the spilling of the blood of Christ. Truly, Jesus had as high an ethic or moral system as any of the founders of other religions. Indeed, it was higher. But Christianity is based upon the teaching that man is a sinner needing a means of atonement for his sins and that in the shedding of the blood of Christ that atonement was made.

Thus, the death of Christ is essential to man's salvation. He had to die if man was to be justified and God remain just. God's law had declared the death penalty for man if he sinned. Since all men sinned, the only way God could be just would be to carry out the death penalty. This He did, but He allowed Jesus to die in man's place (Romans 3:25, 26). Jesus declared that His mission was to die: "From that time forth began Jesus to shew unto his disciples, how that he must go unto Jerusalem, and suffer many things of the elders and chief priests and scribes, and be killed, and be raised again the third day" (Matthew 16:21; compare Mark 8:31; Luke 9:22).

4. The death of Christ was an interest of Heaven. How interesting to note that the heavenly visitors, Moses and Elijah, when they appeared with Jesus on the Mount of Transfiguration, talked about His "decease which he should accomplish at Jerusalem" (Luke 9:31). When John saw the four living creatures and the twenty-four elders, they broke out into a new song praising Christ and saying: "Thou art worthy to take the book, and to open the seals thereof: for thou wast slain, and hast redeemed us to God by the blood out of every kindred, and tongue, and people, and nation" (Revelation 5:9).

There are many misinterpretations of the meaning of the death of Christ. None of them interpret the true significance of His shed blood. These have led to unscriptural concepts of the atonement.

Among the false theories of the atonement has been the view that the death of Christ was a ransom paid to Satan. What is called the *Governmental Theory* held that to maintain respect for His law, God made an example of His hatred of sin in the death of Christ. The *Martyr* or *Example Theory* taught that Christ's death was simply that of a martyr who was killed because He was faithful to His principles. All man needs to do is reform and live His example. The *Moral Influence Theory* holds that Christ suffered in and with His creatures because He took upon Himself human nature. God's love manifested in Christ's death should soften human hearts and influence them toward repentance. The *Accident Theory* would view the death of Christ as unintended. He was killed by people of His day because they rejected His teachings. His death had no more meaning than that of any other good man. Anselm's *Commercial Theory* was nearer truth than any of these. He taught that sin violates the divine honor and deserves infinite punishment. God's honor must be vindicated, and the shed blood of Christ is sufficient to do this and to satisfy the divine claims so that God can pardon sinners.

All of these views miss the vital point of the need for atonement which was fulfilled by the shed blood of Christ. The *Commercial Theory* comes nearest but it too fails. It is the holiness of God which is violated by the sin of man. This is the violation that must be satisfied by the shed blood so that God can pardon sin and accept the sinner. It is in the vicarious suffering of Christ for the sinner that the full meaning of the atonement is found.

II. THE VICARIOUS SUFFERINGS OF CHRIST (Hebrews 9:1-14)

The shedding of His blood was not for His own sins. Peter mentions that He "did no sin, neither was guile found in his mouth" (1 Peter 2:22). The writer of Hebrews wrote that He "was in all points tempted like as we are, yet without sin" (4:15). Thus when it was written that "thou shalt make his soul an offering for sin" (Isaiah 53:10), it was for the sin of others.

The term *vicarious* is used when something is in the stead of another. Thus the sufferings and death of Christ were vicarious because He suffered in our stead. The biblical teaching is always that He died for others. Isaiah emphasized this in his prophecy. He wrote: "He was wounded for our transgressions, he was bruised for our iniquities: the chastisement of our peace was upon him; and with his stripes we are healed. All we like sheep have gone astray; we have turned every one to his own way; and the LORD hath laid on him the iniquity of us all" (53:5, 6). In the New Testament Paul was emphasizing the vicarious nature of His death when he wrote: "Christ died for our sins according to the scriptures" (1 Corinthians 15:3). He also wrote, "Him who knew no sin he made to be sin on our behalf; that we might become the righteousness of God in him" (2 Corinthians 5:21, *American Standard Version*). Over and over these words showing the vicarious nature of His death are given. He Himself said, "The Son of man came not to be ministered unto, but to minister, and to give his life a ransom for many" (Mark 10:45).

The vicarious death of Christ for us is something that we cannot understand. According to the laws of our land, no man would be able to step forward and bear the death penalty of a criminal in his stead. There have been objections to this view, but none so strong but that the Scriptures refute them.

The plain fact of the teaching of Scriptures is that "while we were yet sinners, Christ died for us" (Romans 5:8). It was He who "tasted death for every man" (Hebrews 2:9). God in His wisdom made provision for our salvation through this means. Although we cannot understand how God can collect the debt for our sins through the work of Christ, we accept by faith the Word of God which teaches this. He voluntarily filled our place. The debt for sin will not be collected from us if we accept His shed blood as an atonement for our sins. As someone wrote, "This type substitution is unknown to mere law; it is an operation of grace."

It has been objected that it would be immoral for God to punish an innocent one, that Christ's death is not substitutionary for this reason. This error has a gross weakness in that it is built around the theory that Christ and God are different beings and that God was punishing the innocent Christ for guilty man. But the Scriptures clearly teach that Christ is God Incarnate. The substitute for our sins is God Himself. The Judge of man has chosen to pay the penalty which He has imposed. In the wisdom of God He so planned our salvation that He would pay our penalty. This is not a compulsory penalty paid by Christ but a voluntary one.

If Christ has paid the debt for man's sin, how then can God still collect the debt from sinners? The answer to this question is simple. The one who paid the debt is the Judge. Forgiveness is yet optional with Him. In His divine plan He has chosen to forgive only those who avail themselves of the payment of their debt by faith. This vicarious atonement is sufficient to save all men. It is efficient or effective only to the ones who meet God's conditions: repentance and faith. The sacrifice of Christ for our sins or His obedience does not make ours unnecessary. We become beneficiaries of the atonement by meeting His conditions.

The atonement for our sins may further be described as a satisfaction. The holiness of God has been outraged by sin. For this reason the wrath of God has been revealed against the sins of man and needs to be satisfied. This satisfaction is referred to as *propitiation* by John who said, "Herein is love, not that we loved God, but that he loved us, and sent his Son to be the propitiation for our sins" (1 John 4:10). This word *propitiate* carries with it the concept of appeasing the wrath of God. Jesus said, "He that believeth on the Son hath everlasting life: and he that believeth not the Son shall not see life; but the wrath of God abideth on him" (John 3:36). But then John wrote, "He is the propitiation for our sins: and not for ours only, but also for the sins of the whole world" (1 John 2:2). So the vicarious death of Christ for our sins appeases God's wrath against sin.

His death satisfies also the justice of God. Man's sin broke the law of God and thereby incurred a penalty because of God's displeasure and condemnation. The vicarious death was provided so that "he might be just, and the justifier of him which believeth in Jesus" (Romans 3:26). When the offending sinner claims the satisfaction provided in the death of Christ by repentance and faith, no longer is he liable to condemnation.

Not only is the justice of God satisfied, but all the law of God is satisfied as well. The law required perfect obedience, which man in his fallen state could not yield. Several things are involved here. As our substitute, Christ endured all that the law demanded. His sufferings for our sins and the obedience He rendered to the law released us from its demands. Through His death we are given a righteousness which meets the demands of the law. It is through His righteousness that we are justified and restored to fellowship with God (Romans 3:20-26).

The vicarious suffering and death of Christ has also been related to three other ideas in the New Testament. (1) The first of these is atonement. In the Old Testament the concept of atonement whether for individual trespasses (Leviticus 6:2-7) or national sins (Leviticus 4:13-20) involved the idea of a "covering for sin." Forgiveness or covering of sin was made possible by the death of a substitute. After the death of Christ for us, Paul wrote, "And not only so, but we also joy in God through our Lord Jesus Christ, by whom we have now received the atonement" (Romans 5:11). Thus the Old Testament concept is a preview to what Christ did for us. The death of our substitute is the means by which our guilt is covered (compare Isaiah 38:17; Micah 7:19).

(2) Another thought mentioned in relation to the vicarious death of Christ is the concept of reconciliation. This idea is closely related to propitiation and the latter word is so translated in the King James Version in Hebrews 2:17 where the writer mentions the incarnation as a means for Christ "to make reconciliation [propitiation] for the sins of the people." The ideas are so connected that when propitiation (the divine wrath is satisfied) is accomplished, reconciliation (the offender comes back into favor) results.

Paul writes of this reconciliation when he said, "For if, when we were enemies, we were reconciled to God by the death of his Son, much more, being reconciled, we shall be saved by his life" (Romans 5:10). Probably a good interpretation of what is meant by reconciliation is found in Paul's words which say: He "hath raised us up together, and made us sit together in heavenly places in Christ Jesus" (Ephesians 2:6). In verse 16 of the same chapter he said that the death of Christ was so "that he might reconcile both unto God in one body by the cross, having slain the enmity thereby."

(3) The vicarious death of Christ is described also as a ransom. A ransom is a price paid in order to free one held in bondage. Jesus described His death in this manner when He said, "The Son of Man came not to be ministered unto, but to minister, and to give his life a ransom for many" (Matthew 20:28; Mark 10:45).

Man's sin brought him into bondage to the justice of God. To cancel the claims against man and to free him from bondage to Satan, Christ gave His life as a ransom. Thus it is that Christ came to be identified as our Redeemer (Galatians 3:13; Revelation 5:9).

III. THE VICTORIOUS ACCOMPLISHMENT OF CHRIST (Hebrews 8:1-13; 9:27, 28)

Several thoughts might be brought together under this topic. Surely, the extent of the atonement accomplished by the death of Christ is involved. That victory of Christ also involved His resurrection, ascension, and exaltation. All of these are included in Hebrews 9:28 where the author wrote: "So Christ was once offered to bear the sins of many; and unto them that look for him shall he appear the second time without sin unto salvation."

The extent of the death of Christ has been limited by certain followers of Calvin. While Calvin admitted the universality of the atonement in Christ, certain of his followers interpreted the Scriptures to teach that the death of Christ was for the elect alone. Thus these hyper-Calvinists taught a limited atonement in contrast to the later Arminian theory which taught that it was for the whole world.

It is true that Christ's death was primarily for the elect. Did not Paul say: "We have our hope set on the living God, who is the Saviour of all men, specially of them that believe" (1 Timothy 4:10, *American Standard Version*). As previously mentioned the death of

Christ was sufficient to save all men, but it is efficient only to those who believe. The death of Christ was for all men, but its power to save is only applicable to believers. Thus, there are some Scriptures which would stress the death of Christ for the elect. In Ephesians 5:25 Paul mentioned how that Christ "loved the church, and gave himself for it."

The strong emphasis of the Scriptures, however, is on the fact that Christ died for the sins of the whole world. John the Baptist, upon seeing Jesus, pointed Him out to his own disciples with the words, "Behold the Lamb of God, which taketh away the sin of the world" (John 1:29). Paul, writing to Titus, spoke, saying, "For the grace of God that bringeth salvation hath appeared to all men" (Titus 2:11). And to Timothy he wrote of the Christ "Who gave himself a ransom for all" (1 Timothy 2:6). The writer of Hebrews saw how "that he by the grace of God should taste death for every man" (2:9). And John wrote of Him who died not only for our sins "but also for the sins of the whole world" (1 John 2:2).

Summing up this idea, Strong has written: "His death secured for all men a delay in the execution of the sentence against sin, space for repentance, and the common blessings of life which have been forfeited by transgression; it removed from the mind of God every obstacle to the pardon of the penitent and restoration of the sinner, except his willful opposition to God and rejection of Him; it procured for the unbeliever the powerful incentives to repentance presented in the cross, by means of the preaching of God's servants, and through the work of the Holy Spirit."

The climax of this victorious accomplishment of Christ came in His resurrection. It was the resurrection which guaranteed the validity of all that went before. His teachings that He was the Son of God, His death for our sins, and all His claims to deity were validated by the resurrection.

The resurrection of Christ is the fundamental doctrine of Christianity. Though it is denied by the liberals as an actual event,

Free Will Baptists cling to it as avidly as Paul. He said that "if Christ be not risen," (1) apostolic preaching is vain (1 Corinthians 15:14), (2) believers' faith is in vain (verse 14), (3) the apostles' witness is false (verse 15), (4) the Corinthians are yet in their sins (verse 17), (5) those dead in Christ have perished (verse 18), (6) and believers are of all men most miserable (verse 19). Both Paul and the New Testament church made the resurrection an essential part of Christianity (Acts 2:24; 3:15, 26; 4:10).

Two other facts are important in regard to the resurrection: The resurrection perfects our salvation and makes its application to our lives possible, and His resurrection confirms all the miracles of the Bible. If we disbelieve that miracle, belief in all the others is unnecessary.

The victory of Christ represented by the resurrection is linked to these facts related to our salvation:

1. Our reconciliation (Romans 5:10)

2. The putting away of sin in our lives (Romans 6:10, 11)

3. Our fellowship with Christ (1 Thessalonians 5:10)

4. His Lordship in our lives (Romans 14:9)

5. His heavenly priesthood (Romans 8:34)

6. The future union of Christ with His bride, the church (1 Thessalonians 4:14 ff)

7. The perpetuation of the love of the Father (John 10:17)

Thus, it may be seen that the resurrection is the foundation of all things in the believer's new life in Christ. The resurrection made faith possible. It made all the accomplishments on the cross available to believers.

The victorious accomplishment of Christ involves also His ascension and exaltation. The ascension involves the return of Christ to Heaven in His resurrection body. Although Mark mentions the ascension (16:19), it is Luke who gives the details of that event (Luke 24:50, 51; Acts 1:9). Paul teaches about it in his epistles also (Ephesians 4:8-10; Philippians 2:9; 1 Timothy 3:16). Peter refers to His having "gone into heaven" (1 Peter 3:22).

Liberals deny the actual ascension just as they deny the literal resurrection. But true faith in Christ is dependent upon these facts, for our hope in the return of Christ is based upon His return in the same literal way in which He departed.

The exaltation of Christ is the act of the Father in giving to the ascended Christ the exalted position at His right hand. It included the bestowal of the honor and power due that position. The Scriptures mention several things which are embraced in that exaltation:

1. He was "crowned with glory and honour" (Hebrews 2:9).

2. He received a name that is above every name (Philippians 2:9).

3. Angels, authorities, and powers are subject to Him (1 Peter 3:22).

4. All things are put under Him (Ephesians 1:22).

5. He serves as Head of the Church (Ephesians 1:22; Hebrews 4:14).

As a result of His ascension and exaltation, He is the object of worship for all believers (1 Corinthians 1:2). It is from His position there that He carries on His priestly ministry in Heaven (Hebrews 5:1-10; 6:20; 7:21) and bestows spiritual gifts upon believers (Ephesians 4:8-13).

IV. THE INTERCESSORY WORK OF CHRIST
(Hebrews 7:25-28)

In regard to the intercessory work of Christ, the *Free Will Baptist Treatise* makes the following statement: "Our Lord not only died for our sins, but He arose for our justification, and ascended up to heaven, where, as the only Mediator between God and man, He makes intercession for us until He comes again." This speaks of a very important aspect of Christ's continued relation to the believer.

Although the total work of Christ is sometimes referred to as His intercessory work or mediatorship, this statement deals specifically with that present intercessory work of Christ taking place continually in Heaven. The writer of Hebrews says that "he ever liveth to make intercession for them" (7:25). This is speaking of that continued and effective mediatorship for believers who have come to Him for salvation.

Free Will Baptists do not believe that men are saved and enter into a condition from which they cannot fall. However, they do believe that He who did so much to save us will do even more to keep us saved. Paul, writing to the Romans, said: "God commendeth his love toward us, in that, while we were yet sinners, Christ died for us. Much more then, being now justified by his blood, we shall be saved from wrath through him. For if, when we were enemies, we were reconciled to God by the death of his Son, much more, being reconciled, we shall be saved by his life" (Romans 5:8-10). Thus we see that He is active in regard to our salvation at all times. This is why He can "save to the uttermost them that draw near unto God through him" (*American Standard Version*) because He is involved in this continual work.

This particular work of intercession is seen then to be particularly on behalf of believers in Christ. The great prayer of Christ is recorded in John 17, which is typical of His intercession for believers, for those who are especially united to Him. Paul in his letter to the Romans said, "Who is he that condemneth? It is Christ that died, yea rather, that is risen again, who is even at the right hand of God, who also maketh intercession for us" (8:34). This is similar to the thought given by the writer of Hebrews who wrote that "Christ is not entered into the holy places made with hands, which are the figures of the true; but into heaven itself, now to appear in the presence of God for us" (9:24).

The believer is saved, but his condition is of such a nature that he needs the continual intercession of Christ on his behalf. The several Scriptures above refer to the specific intercession of Christ, but we may be sure that His intercession for us is related to that intercession of the Holy Spirit for us which is mentioned by Paul. Of that intercession Paul wrote: "Likewise the Spirit also helpeth our infirmities: for we know not what we should pray for as we ought: but the Spirit itself maketh intercession for us with groanings which cannot be uttered" (Romans 8:26).

Believers who sin will find the intercession of Christ especially effective in their lives. The specific admonition of the Scriptures to believers is "sin not." But the fatherly John recognizing the weaknesses in believers wrote a prescription to believers, "if any man sin." To those who do sin, he said, "We have an advocate with the Father, Jesus Christ the righteous: And he is the propitiation for our sins: and not for ours only, but also for the sins of the whole world" (1 John 2:1, 2). Thus he described to us the great Advocate or Intercessor who is daily concerned with the continuance of our salvation. The writer of Hebrews described Him not only as the "author of our salvation," but also as its finisher.

Chapter Four

5

The Holy Spirit, His Work and Person

BACKGROUND

The apostles and other New Testament Christians, who had been taught all their lives that there was one God, had no trouble in recognizing that Jesus was divine. When Paul became convinced that Jesus was indeed alive, he immediately began to proclaim the divine Sonship of Jesus.

Neither did the New Testament Christians have any difficulty in recognizing that the Holy Spirit was divine. They merely accepted the fact and never bothered themselves about the doctrine.

It was in later times when men began to question the doctrine of the Trinity; and through examination and comparisons of various portions of Scripture, Bible scholars have formulated what is called the Doctrine of the Holy Spirit.

Every Christian should be careful to avoid either extreme on the doctrine of the Holy Spirit—the emotional outbursts attributed by some as evidence of the presence of the Holy Spirit and the avoidance of any mention of the Holy Spirit for fear of being classified as a fanatic. It would be well to remember that nearly any extreme is wrong.

There is a new interest being shown in the so-called tongues doctrine in relation to the Holy Spirit. It would be well to point out that the Bible predicts the cessation of tongues (1 Corinthians 13:8), and in verse 13 indicates that already such was the case for "now abideth [remaineth] faith, hope, charity, these three; but the greatest of these is charity." In 1 Corinthians 12:31 Paul writes that the more excellent way (better than tongues, miracles, etc.) is the way of love.

Spirituality is not to be measured by emotional outbursts but by the consistent Christian life of the believer.

OUTLINE

    I. **The Holy Spirit As a Personality (John 16:1-15)**

    II. **The Work of the Holy Spirit (Acts 1:3-8; 2:1-21; 13:1-5)**

    III. **The Holy Spirit in the Trinity (1 John 5:6-9)**

INTRODUCTION

Believers are usually less acquainted with the Holy Spirit than with either of the members of the Holy Trinity. Actually, the case should be the other way around. The Holy Spirit is that divine Person of whom the believer should have constant knowledge and awareness. Jesus was on earth and known among men, but when He went away He sent the other Comforter so that believers could ever live with the presence of God in their lives. The Holy Spirit is that Comforter and was the fulfilment of "the promise of the Father" to believers.

Fanaticism has arisen in many circles regarding the presence of the Holy Spirit in lives and in regard to what constitutes "evidence" of the Holy Spirit. Some have insisted that a gift of speaking in unknown tongues is the only real evidence of the gift of the

Spirit. Others look for outward evidences of "spirituality," which they associate with the presence of the Holy Spirit in a life. It is probably such fanaticism which has filled many in the churches with a strange fear of the Holy Spirit.

In this study of the Holy Spirit each of us should strive to find some concept of the Spirit which will enable us to better understand the work of the Holy Spirit and to yield greater obedience to Him.

I. THE HOLY SPIRIT AS A PERSONALITY
(John 16:1.15)

The Holy Spirit is a personal being. Somehow or other in contrast to the Father and the Son some people have a feeling that the Holy Spirit is impersonal. Probably the use of the term *ghost* or *spirit* in His name yields somewhat of a concept that is easier to be impersonalized than either that of Father or Son. But as the *Treatise* states: "The Scriptures ascribe to the Holy Spirit the acts and attributes of an intelligent being. He guides, knows, moves, gives information, commands, forbids, sends forth, reproves, and can be sinned against."

Probably the secret and mystical acts of the Holy Spirit add to this feeling of His being impersonal. Because His work is the invisible working in the hearts of men, it is easy to think of Him as an influence or power rather than a personal being. In fact, there are those who prefer to view Him merely as the manifestation of the divine nature or the influence of God.

Even the names given to the Holy Spirit suggest impersonality. Spirit or ghost (both are translations of the same Greek term) can also be translated breath, wind, or power. The symbols which are used of the Spirit are likewise of an impersonal nature. Jesus compared the movement of the Spirit in His work to the wind (John

3:8). His coming at Pentecost is stated in terms describing "tongues like as of fire" (Acts 2:3) or "a rushing mighty wind" (2:2).

The term *spirit* itself is neuter. The *Authorized Version* uses the neuter pronoun "itself" when speaking of the Holy Spirit but this is corrected in the *Revised (American Standard) Version* (Romans 8:16, 26).

The proofs for the personality of the Holy Spirit are numerous. In contrast to what has been said, it should be noted that the Holy Spirit is given names which indicate personality. Probably the most significant one is given by Jesus who called Him the Comforter (John 14:16; 16:7). This same word is used of Christ in 1 John 2:1 (*advocate* in the Greek is the same as *comforter*). Did not Jesus in His original statement speak of "another" Comforter? No influence or impersonal power could fill such a position.

Although the neuter pronoun is used of the Holy Spirit, there are more times that the masculine personal pronoun is used when it refers to Him. For example, it is used of Him twelve times in John 16:7, 8, 13-15. The word *spirit* is neuter and should demand a neuter pronoun, but in these instances it specifically is not used.

Another evidence of personality is found in the identification of the Holy Spirit with the Father and Son. The baptismal formula given by Jesus in Matthew 28:19 would almost demand identification of the Spirit as a Person: "in the name of the Father, and of the Son, and of the Holy Ghost." Since it is in the "name" rather than "names," the implication is that all three are equal persons. The same argument might be used for Paul's apostolic benediction. In it he wished upon the Corinthians the blessings of "the grace of the Lord Jesus Christ, and the love of God, and the communion of the Holy Ghost" (2 Corinthians 13:14). Again the emphasis is of such a nature that it implies the equality of three Persons.

The Holy Spirit is identified with Christians in a way that presupposes a person rather than an influence. Paul, speaking in Acts

15:28, said, "For it seemed good to the Holy Ghost, and to us, to lay upon you no greater burden than these necessary things." This could not be said of a mere influence. In Romans 15:13 Paul wished upon the Romans "that ye may abound in hope, through the power of the Holy Ghost." If the Holy Spirit is only a power or influence, this would have to read, "through the power of the power." This makes the passage meaningless, even absurd.

Personal characteristics are ascribed to the Holy Spirit. In 1 Peter 1:11 the Holy Spirit is seen possessing knowledge of the deep things of God, even a foreknowledge of the sufferings of Christ. Paul understood that the Spirit of God had a knowledge of the most profound truths of God (1 Corinthians 2:10, 11). Mind is a characteristic of truth, and the Word gives such to the Holy Spirit (Romans 8:27). Spiritual gifts are received from the Holy Spirit according to Paul (1 Corinthians 12:4, 11).

Probably one of the strongest evidences of personality in the Holy Spirit is found in the acts which He did. The Holy Spirit speaks as is recorded in Revelation 2:7 which says: "He that hath an ear, let him hear what the Spirit saith unto the churches." The Spirit communicated to the apostles the fact that they were not to go into Bithynia (Acts 16:7). It was the Holy Spirit who first directed Paul and Barnabas on their missionary journey, saying to the church at Antioch, "Separate me Barnabas and Saul for the work whereunto I have called them" (Acts 13:2). The Spirit makes intercession for believers in a way that only a person could (Romans 8:26).

Yet another fact demonstrating personality in the Holy Spirit is His susceptibility to personal treatment. The sin against the Holy Ghost was set forth by Jesus as more grievous than sin against Him who was the Son of God. Jesus said, "All manner of sin and blasphemy shall be forgiven unto men: but the blasphemy against the Holy Ghost shall not be forgiven unto men" (Matthew 12:31). This is probably the same as "despite unto the Spirit of grace" mentioned by the author of Hebrews (10:29). It is probably the sin for which John said, "I do not say that he shall pray for it" (1 John 5:16).

The Holy Spirit by bad personal treatment may also be grieved. Paul warned in Ephesians 4:30: "And grieve not the holy Spirit of God, whereby ye are sealed unto the day of redemption." Peter must have thought that the Holy Spirit was a Person for he sensed He could be lied to. In Acts 5:3 he accused Ananias of such a thing. In the same event he accused this man and Sapphira, his wife, of agreeing together "to tempt the Spirit of the Lord" (5:9).

In all these examples and throughout the New Testament the Holy Spirit is pictured as a vital, living Person in inter-personal relationships. But, the Holy Spirit is not just a Person. He is a divine Person possessing all the characteristics of deity.

The *Free Will Baptist Treatise* teaches this by saying: "The attributes of God are ascribed to the Holy Spirit." The Bible does not go to as great an extent in describing these attributes for the Holy Spirit as it does in the case of the Father, but it does not need to do so. The Holy Spirit is God and thus would bear all the attributes elsewhere ascribed to the Godhead. The Holy Spirit is described as being eternal. In Hebrews 9:14 He is referred to as "the eternal Spirit." The psalmist goes to a great extent to describe the omnipresence of the Spirit of God in Psalm 139:7-10. The Holy Spirit is omnipotent for in Luke 1:35 His power is made parallel with "the power of the Highest." His omniscience is brought out in 1 Corinthians 2:10, 11.

The Scriptures also ascribe divine works to the Holy Spirit. The *Treatise* lists these as: "creation, inspiration, giving of life, and sanctification." In Genesis 1:2 the writer says, "And the Spirit of God moved upon the face of the waters." This activity of the Spirit in creation also seems to be referred to in Psalm 104:30. And Job reported, "The Spirit of God hath made me, and the breath of the Almighty hath given me life" (33:4).

It was Peter who wrote of the activity of the Spirit in the inspiration of the Scriptures. He said that "holy men of God spake as they were moved by the Holy Ghost" (2 Peter 1:21). To Nicodemus, Jesus described the work of the Holy Spirit in the New Birth. Being "born again" (John 3:3) is made synonymous with being "born of the Spirit" (3:5, 6, 8).

The Spirit has the power to bestow life. It was by the power of the Spirit that Christ was raised and through whom eternal life is transmitted to believers (Romans 8:11). Peter also refers to a quickening "by the Spirit" (1 Peter 3:18). Related to this is the work of sanctification mentioned by Paul (1 Corinthians 6:11).

The association of the Holy Spirit with the Father and Son in the Trinity is another evidence of His deity. The *Treatise* states that "the conclusion is that the Holy Spirit is in reality God and one with the Father in all divine perfections." The Great Commission given "in the name of the Father, and of the Son, and of the Holy Ghost" (Matthew 28:19) would seem absurd if the Holy Spirit were not a divine Person on an equality with the Father and the Son. Likewise, the apostolic benediction would appear absurd if Jesus Christ, God, and the Holy Ghost (2 Corinthians 13:14) were not equal in the Godhead.

The Holy Spirit is expressly called God by the Scriptures. In Isaiah 6:8-10 the passage refers to God but when used by Paul in Acts 28:25-27 it is made to refer to the Holy Spirit. This is true also of Exodus 16:7, which is used in this manner of the Holy Spirit in Hebrews 3:7-9. In Acts 5:3, 4 the Holy Spirit is specifically called God. It is inferred that the Holy Ghost and the Lord are the same by the author of the book of Hebrews (10:15).

In the passage given for the basis of this study (John 16:1-15), Jesus gave an introduction to the Holy Spirit. Much that relates to the work of the Holy Spirit is described there and will be brought out in the next section dealing with the work of the Holy Spirit.

However, this passage should be carefully studied for its many implications regarding the personality of the Holy Spirit.

II. THE WORK OF THE HOLY SPIRIT
(Acts 1:3-8; 2:1-21; 13:1.5)

In John 16:1-15 Jesus mentioned many things that the Holy Spirit would do.

1. "He will reprove the world of sin, and of righteousness, and of judgment" (verse 8).

2. "He will guide you into all truth" (verse 13).

3. "He shall not speak of himself; but whatsoever he shall hear, that shall he speak" (verse 13).

4. "He will shew you things to come" (verse 13).

5. "He shall glorify me" (verse 14).

In these passages from Acts other works of the Holy Spirit are pointed out:

1. He shall bestow power upon believers so that they may be witnesses (1:3-8).

2. Special power for preaching the Word of God would come through Him (Acts 2:1-21).

3. Call to missionary service would come from the Holy Spirit (Acts 13:1-2).

4. Leadership in missionary activity would come from the Holy Spirit (13:3-5).

The work of the Holy Spirit in creation, inspiration, and giving of life has already been mentioned. The continuing work of the Holy Spirit is the main interest of this study now. Although the agency of the Spirit is seen in creation, this thought will not be pursued. However, there is some evidence that the power of the Spirit continues in the preservation of nature. For example, Isaiah wrote: "The grass withereth, the flower fadeth: because the spirit of the LORD bloweth upon it" (40:7).

The Holy Spirit continues to work in relation to all of humanity. This is what Jesus meant when He spoke of the Holy Spirit convincing men in regard to sin, righteousness, and judgment (John 16:8). Explaining this convincing of the world in relation to each of the three things mentioned, Jesus said: "Of sin, because they believe not on me; of righteousness, because I go to my Father, and ye see me no more; of judgment, because the prince of this world is judged" (John 16:9-11). Of these three great facts the Holy Spirit is constantly bearing witness to the world. This was in keeping with the testimony of Christ when He said: "But when the Comforter is come, whom I will send unto you from the Father, even the Spirit of truth, which proceedeth from the Father, he shall testify of me" (John 15:26).

It would appear that much of the testimony of the Spirit would be through believers. The witness of the two is linked in Acts 5:32 and in John 15:26, 27.

It is in relation to the believer that the Holy Spirit especially works. It was to believers that the Comforter was promised, for Jesus said to His disciples, "And I will pray the Father, and he shall give you another Comforter, that he may abide with you for ever; Even the Spirit of truth; whom the world cannot receive, because it seeth him not, neither knoweth him: but ye know him; for he dwelleth with you, and shall be in you" (John 14:16, 17). It was to believers that Jesus said, "He shall teach you all things, and bring all things to your remembrance, whatsoever I have said unto you" (John 14:26).

The relation to the believer started, however, just as it started with all humanity. The Holy Spirit had to first convince or convict the believer of sin while he was yet in the world. But anyone who is convinced of his sin and appropriates the work of Christ in his life finds that the Holy Spirit becomes an ever-present reality in his life. It is through this that the words of Jesus become true that "I am in my Father, and ye in me, and I in you" (John 14:20).

The beginning work of the Holy Spirit in the life of the believer is regeneration. This was the work described by Jesus to Nicodemus in the words, "be born again" (John 3:3). To him Jesus said, "Except a man be born of water and of the Spirit, he cannot enter into the kingdom of God" (3:5). This describes man's physical birth and his spiritual birth, the results of each being described in the next verse. Paul, writing to Titus, described this new birth or regeneration as the "renewing of the Holy Ghost" (Titus 3:5). The Holy Spirit is the active agent in bringing renewed spiritual life to the soul that is dead in trespasses and sin. Elsewhere Jesus showed how that it is the Spirit who gives life when He said, "It is the spirit that quickeneth" (John 6:63).

At the time of regeneration when the believer is brought to new life in Christ, the Holy Spirit indwells the believer. This indwelling was described by Paul when he wrote: "But ye are not in the flesh, but in the Spirit, if so be that the Spirit of God dwell in you" (Romans 8:9). And elsewhere he said, "Your body is the temple of the Holy Ghost which is in you" (1 Corinthians 6:19). There are those who teach the mistaken doctrine that you may be saved and later filled with the Holy Spirit, but it is the coming of the Holy Spirit which brings life and is synonymous with spiritual life. So every believer, no matter how weak or immature, is enlivened by the presence of the Holy Spirit which dwells within him. This is why Paul said, "Now if any man have not the Spirit of Christ, he is none of his" (Romans 8:9). Actually the believer's witness and life depends upon this residence of the Spirit for "no man can say that Jesus is the Lord, but by the Holy Ghost" (1 Corinthians 12:3).

This indwelling of the Spirit becomes the means of assurance of salvation to the believer. Paul wrote to the Ephesian believers that "after that ye believed, ye were sealed with that holy Spirit of promise, which is the earnest of our inheritance" (1:13, 14). Those who teach the doctrine of eternal security see the Holy Spirit as a seal on salvation, a seal that cannot be broken. Paul's picture seems to be somewhat different to this. In calling the Holy Spirit the "earnest" of our salvation, he appears to be giving the concept of a down payment which acts as security. The sealing by the Holy Spirit, His presence in a life, is evidence of (1) ownership by God, and (2) likeness to God (2 Timothy 2:19-21). Through the presence of the Holy Spirit in his life, the believer is "sealed unto the day of redemption" (Ephesians 4:30).

The assurance to the believer is derived from the felt presence of the Holy Spirit. Paul describes this assurance as "the Spirit of adoption, whereby we cry, Abba, Father" (Romans 8:15). It is "because ye are sons, God hath sent forth the Spirit of his Son into your hearts, crying, Abba, Father." Then Paul tells us, "The Spirit itself beareth witness with our spirit, that we are the children of God" (Romans 8:16). How wonderful to know that we are saved! God does not leave us in doubt but gives us assurance through the Holy Spirit.

There are times that the believer receives a special infilling of the Holy Spirit. This took place at Pentecost when the believers "were all filled with the Holy Ghost" (Acts 2:4). This occasion called for a special demonstration of power. This was given through believers who, though they were all of one language, spoke in a tongue understood by people from many language areas. Paul urged believers to "be filled with the Spirit" (Ephesians 5:18). Although these were already indwelt by the Spirit, special power for special occasions was to be sought. The believers who were filled at Pentecost were filled again when another special need arose (Acts 4:31). All believers possess the Spirit but should seek a filling by the Spirit whenever faced with special tasks.

The Holy Spirit empowers the believer to live the spiritual life and to labor in the service of the Lord. Because the believer has been changed, "we are debtors, not to the flesh, to live after the flesh" (Romans 8:12). Through the Spirit we are to "mortify the deeds of the body" (Romans 8:13) that we might live. Following the Spirit results in the fruit of the Spirit being produced in one's life. This "fruit" consists of the graces: love, joy, peace, longsuffering, gentleness, goodness, meekness, faith, temperance (Galatians 5:22, 23).

The total walk of the believer should be mapped by the Holy Spirit. For this reason Paul urges us to "walk in the Spirit" (Galatians 5:16). The direction of the Spirit should be depended on especially when one is called upon to give a witness for Christ under difficult circumstances.

The Holy Spirit anoints the believer for knowledge and teaching. John said, "But the anointing which ye have received of him abideth in you, and ye need not that any man teach you: but as the same anointing teacheth you of all things, and is truth, and is no lie, and even as it hath taught you, ye shall abide in him" (1 John 2:27). Paul discussed this spiritual discernment that comes to believers because of the presence of the Spirit in their lives (1 Corinthians 2:9-14).

The relation of the Holy Spirit to the Scriptures has already been mentioned briefly. Paul, writing to Timothy, described the Scriptures as being "God-breathed" (2 Timothy 3:16). Peter further developed this thought by saying that "holy men of God spake as they were moved by the Holy Ghost" (2 Peter 1:21). The writing of the New Testament was probably anticipated by Jesus when He said, "Howbeit when he, the Spirit of truth, is come, he will guide you into all truth: . . . and he will shew you things to come" (John 16:13).

This guidance of the Holy Spirit is also found in His help as an interpreter of Scriptures. Instead of inspiration, His aid to the believers in interpreting the Scriptures is usually referred to as illumination. Jesus said, "He shall receive of mine, and shall shew it unto you" (John 16:14). This is why He is called the "spirit of wisdom and revelation" (Ephesians 1:17).

The Holy Spirit is equal with the other members of the Godhead. Each believer should render Him the same honor that he bestows upon each of the other two. Our Comforter should be dear to us and one to whom we resort for constant leadership.

III. THE HOLY SPIRIT IN THE TRINITY
(1 John 5:6-9)

Distinctions in the Godhead are introduced very early in the Scriptures. The first two verses of the book of Genesis gives a distinction between God (the Father) and the Holy Spirit. "God created the world" but the Holy Spirit was involved in that creation for "the Spirit of God moved upon the face of the waters" (Genesis 1:2). This distinction is maintained in Genesis 6:3 where the Lord said, "My spirit shall not always strive with man." Of course, these distinctions are developed to the point that they reveal the Trinity in later Scriptures, especially with the coming of the Son of God as Messiah.

The doctrine of the Trinity is not in conflict with the teaching that there is one God. This doctrine teaches that there are three Persons in the one divine essence. Although there are no natural analogies to compare with the Trinity, the doctrine is accepted because the Scriptures teach it.

These distinctions in the Godhead are eternal and were not just adaptations for means of manifestation. The Holy Spirit was present in the beginning" (Genesis 1:2). So the Son was present also (John 1:1).

Although the word *person* is used with some reserve, the concept of distinction needs to be maintained. The term should not be used in an exclusive sense of three separate individuals. This leads to a doctrine of three Gods, which is definitely not biblical.

The distinction is mainly of office or function. The Father is presented as the source and origin of all things. The Son is the medium of the outgoing energy of God. It is through the Son that God is manifested: "No man hath seen God at any time; the only begotten Son, which is in the bosom of the Father, he hath declared him" (John 1:18). Every manifestation seen by human eyes was the second person of the Godhead. The Holy Spirit has the work of completing all things. However, the work of all three should be viewed as including the work of the other. All were involved in Creation; likewise all were involved in the plan of salvation.

In one sense, all work in and through each other. At any time the conception is pressed that one works and then the other two great distinctions begin to emerge. The work of the Son is as much the work of God as that of the Father. The same may be said of the work of the Holy Spirit.

Different terms have been used to describe the relations within the Godhead. Of course, the Unitarians have so depreciated the position of the Holy Spirit that He is not considered a person of the Godhead. They and other liberals have also compromised the position of Christ until He is made less than God and in some instances only a man. The term *generation* is usually used of the relation of the Father and the Son. The Lord said through the psalmist, "This day have I begotten thee" (Psalm 2:7). "This day," of course, is the universal presence of God.

The term *possession* is used to describe the relation of the Holy Spirit to the Father and the Son. The split between the Roman Catholic Church and the Greek Orthodox Church came about over the question of whether the Holy Spirit proceeded from the Father or from both Father and Son. Jesus tells us that "the Father will send [the Comforter] in my name" (John 14:26). In the next chapter He speaks of "the Spirit of truth, which proceedeth from the Father" (15:26) but that "I will send [Him] unto you from the Father" (compare also Acts 2:33 and Hebrews 9:14).

The relation of the Holy Spirit to Christ is mentioned in many Scriptures: (1) Luke tells us that Christ was conceived by the Holy Spirit (1:35). The Holy Spirit was vitally related to His birth. (2) Jesus was led by the Spirit. Matthew relates how He was "led up of the Spirit into the wilderness to be tempted of the devil" (4:1). (3) Christ's anointing for service was with the Holy Spirit: "God anointed Jesus of Nazareth with the Holy Ghost and with power" (Acts 10:38). (4) Jesus was crucified in the power of the Holy Spirit. The writer of Hebrews speaks of Christ "who through the eternal Spirit offered himself without spot to God" (9:14). (5) But He was also raised and "declared to be the Son of God with power, according to the spirit of holiness" (Romans 1:4; see also 8:11). (6) After His resurrection Jesus "through the Holy Ghost" gave commandments unto the apostles (Acts 1:2). (7) Jesus, who before His death promised the Holy Spirit to believers, is seen as the bestower of the Holy Spirit in Acts 2:33.

The work of the Holy Spirit is more involved than just in relation to individual believers. The Holy Spirit works also through the body of believers in the Church. Actually, the Church is constituted or formed because the Holy Spirit brings believers into a relationship in Jesus Christ. The Church is a body of men who have been regenerated by the power of the Spirit. All the members of the Church share in common the fact that they have been quickened from the old life by the power of the Spirit.

Such a body which has its life through the Spirit is then led and directed by that Spirit (Ephesians 5:18-20). Thus the Church is a spiritual body and not a social organization. Its life and existence is maintained as its members sustain a relationship to Christ through the Holy Spirit. A church which moves without the direction of the Spirit is no true church.

Chapter Five

6

Doctrines of Salvation

BACKGROUND

Many denominations can find grounds for fellowship around the correct interpretation of the doctrine of salvation. If they teach the plan of salvation correctly, we can acknowledge them as fellow Christians. Certainly, it is in this area that we can decide upon fellowship and cooperation.

Even though many may be right about the plan of salvation, there are differences of opinion regarding the doctrines adhering to the plan of salvation. These differences are sometimes so great as to prevent close fellowship. When such is the case, it is best for each to go his separate way.

Because of the wide variety of opinions, it is good for the Christian to be grounded in these truths presented in today's lesson.

This lesson is one of utmost importance. If one is not in a right relationship with God, all of his other ideas will be useless.

Surely there needs to be no encouragement to the teacher to study this chapter prayerfully. As a spiritual leader the teacher should be able to discuss these doctrines intelligently. Here is a chance to become more fully grounded in the Word of God.

Among Protestants, justification by faith is a cardinal doctrine. Repentance, long emphasized by many, is not being considered as important; neither is justification by faith. There is a need to reemphasize the doctrines in this chapter. Will you help?

OUTLINE

I. Salvation Is Possible for All (Acts 17:22-31)
II. Repentance Is Demanded of All (2 Corinthians 7:8-10)
III. Faith Is Required in Salvation (Hebrews 11:1-6)
IV. Regeneration Is the Result of Repentance and Faith (John 3:1-8)
V. Justification and Sanctification Are By-Products of Regeneration (Romans 5:1-11)

INTRODUCTION

The *Free Will Baptist Treatise* devotes six chapters to subjects concerned with salvation. From nature and other means we can learn some things about God. But it is only from the revealed Word of God that we can learn that God has a redemptive pur pose for His creation and the nature of the salvation which God offers. The main import of all the Scriptures is that man is a creation of God who is out of fellowship with his Maker. However, God has made provision for man's salvation if he will meet the conditions God has revealed to him.

It was the work of Christ which made provision for man's salvation, and the doctrines of salvation dealt with in this lesson will describe the application of the work of Christ to the lives of individuals. The universality of the provision of salvation will be discussed, as well as faith and repentance as the conditions of salvation. Following this, regeneration, justification, and sanctification will be described.

I. SALVATION IS POSSIBLE FOR ALL
(Acts 17:22-31)

One of the beliefs with which the early apostles of Christ had to contend with in their ministry was the belief in many gods. People believed that the many gods were local and were dominant over certain areas of the country. When Paul reached Athens with the gospel, he found the people eager to please all the gods they could. Their pantheon of gods included all those of which they had heard. Thus Athens was "wholly given to idolatry" (Acts 17:16). Paul accused them of being "too superstitious" (verse 22) or overly religious. It was then that Paul introduced them to the one God who had created all things (verse 24) and who commanded "all men every where to repent" (verse 30). This is a universal call which goes out to all men.

This command or call to repent is described in the *Treatise* thusly: "The call of the Gospel is co-extensive with the atonement to all men, both by the word and strivings of the Spirit, so that salvation is rendered equally possible to all; and if any fail of eternal life, the fault is wholly his own."

The call of God is the same as the call of the gospel. This call of God is sometimes referred to as the doctrine of vocation. Peter in his sermon at Pentecost referred to this call of God when he said, "The promise is unto you, and to your children, and to all that are afar off, even as many as the Lord our God shall call" (Acts 2:39). This call of God is His way of meeting man. God makes His voice heard by the conscience of man. It is always God who initiates the meeting with man by issuing the call to him. Adam was not seeking God; in fact, he was hiding from God until he "heard the voice of the LORD God" (Genesis 3:8).

The encounter of Adam with God initiated a string of encounters with men that has continued to this day. In God's call He reveals Himself to man and causes man to realize his need. The

81

Word of God is a record of God calling man. Christ as the Word of God is the incarnation of the call of God to man. He, too, revealed the call as universal. He said on one occasion, "And I, if I be lifted up from the earth, will draw all men unto me" (John 12:32). Jesus came because "God so loved the world, that he gave his only begotten Son, that whosoever believeth in him should not perish, but have everlasting life" (John 3:16).

The *Treatise* also views the call of God as universal when it states it to be "co-extensive with the atonement to all men." Calvinism has taught a limited atonement, that it was for the elect alone. We believe the Scriptures teach that the atonement is unlimited. The blood of Christ was shed for all men. The call to partake in this atonement is likewise universal. Paul wrote, "God hath concluded them all in unbelief, that he might have mercy upon all" (Romans 11:32). This is why Jesus issued the gospel call to all who "labour and are heavy laden" (Matthew 11:28). The invitation is always open to "whosoever will" (John 3:16; Revelation 22:17). God is "not willing that any should perish, but that all should come to repentance" (2 Peter 3:9). So God not only desires to save all but extends help to all who will receive Him.

God's universal call is not irresistible. It is true that God "will have all men to be saved, and to come unto the knowledge of the truth" (1 Timothy 2:4), but salvation for the individual depends upon his response to the call of God: "Except ye repent, ye shall all likewise perish" (Luke 13:3, 5). When Jesus said, "Many are called, but few are chosen," He was probably referring to this very fact. The "chosen" ones are those who personally respond to the call. Jesus likewise was illustrating this same fact in the story of the Wedding Supper. One guest among those who were called refused to go to the dressing room and put on the wedding garment which was provided according to the custom for him. Because he refused the proper wedding garment, he was rejected from the number who attended the feast.

Men are "called to be saints" (Romans 1:7). Response to God's call will provide a means for entering into the plan of God whereby one becomes a saint. So the calling of God is a saving invitation. One is called from a life of sin into salvation.

Paul wrote to the Romans that they had been "called of Jesus Christ" (Romans 1:6). In this call our Lord calls us to Himself and fellowship with God the Father. Response to the call initiates the believer into a partaking of the blessings of salvation. Paul, writing to the church at Thessalonica, said that God "hath called you unto his kingdom and glory" (1 Thessalonians 2:12). This is His spiritual kingdom and a share in the glory of God. The call to His glory is also mentioned in his second letter to the Thessalonians. There, Paul wrote, "He called you by our gospel, to the obtaining of the glory of our Lord Jesus Christ" (2:14).

God also calls us to an inheritance. The "promise of eternal inheritance" is mentioned by the writer of Hebrews (9:15). Paul called it "an inheritance among all them which are sanctified" (Acts 20:32). Peter said that it was "an inheritance incorruptible, and undefiled, and that fadeth not away, reserved in heaven for you" (1 Peter 1:4). Paul speaks of "the riches of the glory of his inheritance in the saints" (Ephesians 1:18).

Elsewhere we are told that we are called by God "unto the fellowship of his Son Jesus Christ our Lord" (1 Corinthians 1:9). We are called to be possessors of "the peace of God" (Colossians 3:15). What we are called into is also called "liberty" or "freedom" in Galatians 5:13. Both Paul and Peter say that we are called into a holy life (1 Thessalonians 4:7; 1 Peter 1:15).

That salvation's call was to all men is revealed in the Old Testament as well as in the New Testament. It is interesting to read of how people outside the covenant people entered by faith into the divine relationship. In the Old Testament the entrance of Gentile women into the very genealogy of the Messiah is given special note. Among these were Rahab the harlot (Hebrews 11:31; James 2:25) and Ruth (Ruth 4:17).

The message of the prophets contained teachings that showed the universality of God's provision of salvation. Isaiah proclaimed such a message in these words: "Look unto me, and be ye saved, all the ends of the earth: for I am God, and there is none else" (45:22). The book of Jonah is a commentary on the universality of God's provision of salvation. The prophet Jonah in describing his own narrowness of the concept of God's plan of salvation is typical of the atttitude of the nation. He told his story to help his people realize that God loved all people and not Israel alone.

The means of that universal call of God is described in the *Treatise* as being both "the word and the strivings of the Spirit." In the Word of God is found the gospel, the good news of salvation. It is the revelation of how God intends to save men from their sins. When men hear the Word of God, the Holy Spirit convinces them of its truth and urges man to accept the Savior revealed in the Word. But God also uses human instrumentality. Every believer is to be a witness by giving his testimony of what Christ has done in his life. The Great Commission instructs every believer to "Go ye therefore, and teach all nations . . . to observe all things whatsoever I have commanded you" (Matthew 28:19, 20).

II. REPENTANCE IS DEMANDED OF ALL
(2 Corinthians 7:8-10)

That repentance is demanded of all men is a doctrine which cannot be overestimated. The biblical doctrine is that man is lost: "All have sinned, and come short of the glory of God" (Romans 3:23). Related to this fact and God's provision of salvation is the teaching that God requires certain things of man if he is to have restored fellowship with God and be saved. Those requirements on man's part are repentance and faith.

The importance of the doctrine of repentance is shown in varied ways. The forerunner of Christ, John the Baptist, began his public ministry with and had as the burden of his ministry the preaching of repentance. To high and low alike, he said, "Repent ye: for the kingdom of heaven is at hand" (Matthew 3:2, compare also 3:8-11).

Jesus took up this same message and made it the key to His preaching (Matthew 4:17). It seems to have remained a central issue in his preaching for on one occasion in Jerusalem He declared, "Except ye repent, ye shall all likewise perish" (Luke 13:3, 5). When He gave instructions to the seventy disciples which went before Him, He commanded them to preach "that men should repent" (Mark 6:12). Related to the Great Commission was the fact that "repentance and remission of sins should be preached in his name among all nations, beginning at Jerusalem" (Luke 24:47).

The apostles did just what Jesus said. In his great sermon at Pentecost, Peter said, "Repent, and be baptized every one of you in the name of Jesus Christ for the remission of sins" (Acts 2:38). Paul went about "testifying both to the Jews, and also to the Greeks, repentance toward God, and faith toward our Lord Jesus Christ" (Acts 20:21). At Athens he preached that God "now commandeth all men every where to repent" (Acts 17:30).

Repentance comes from a Greek word which means "to change the mind." Gospel repentance calls for a change of one's mind, thought, purpose, and views regarding God and spiritual things. For the sinner it is to realize that he is going in the wrong direction and to change his course of life to conform to the ways of God. All of this involves the negative aspects of repentance as one becomes so convicted of his wrong way of life that he begins to acknowledge the error of his way and to detest the old life.

There are positive aspects to repentance also. Not only must the sinner forsake the old way of life, but he must redirect his whole being toward conformity to a new way of life. It is not enough just to be convicted of sin or emotionally disturbed about one's condition. Repentance implies a change from one way to another. Some have described the four elements in repentance as (1) conviction, (2) contrition, (3) confession, and (4) a forsaking of the old way. The forsaking of the old way of life would consist also of a turning to the new way of life in Christ.

Repentance involves the mind, the emotions, and the will. There is a change of mind. One's attitude and views toward sin and righteousness are reversed. The emotions are always involved in true repentance (2 Corinthians 7:9). Feelings, involving sorrow of heart for one's condition and joy at release from sin's bondage, are always present in repentance. The intellectual and emotional elements are incomplete, however, without the act of the will. The Prodigal Son said, "I will arise and go to my father" (Luke 15:18). So must the sinner by an act of the will come to the Heavenly Father who offers him salvation.

Repentance is man's part in salvation, but even repentance is a gift of God. It is aroused in man as he hears the gospel preached. That it is a divine gift is seen in the words of Peter who said, "Then hath God also to the Gentiles granted repentance unto life" (Acts 11:18). And Paul, writing to Timothy, said, ". . . God peradventure will give them repentance to the acknowledging of the truth" (2 Timothy 2:25).

Several means are used to bring men to repentance. In the previous paragraph the preaching of the gospel was mentioned as a means to arouse man to repentance. Besides human witness the convicting power of the Holy Spirit is needed to convince man of his need to repent. Sometimes men repent because they observe the goodness of God in their lives (Romans 2:4). At other times it takes chastisements to bring wanderers back to the fold (Hebrews 12:6, 10, 11; Revelation 3:19). All of these means are but the fruit of the love of God. God brings His influences to bear upon the sinner, but it is the sinner who chooses to go on in his own way or to turn in repentance to God.

It is thrilling to read of the results of repentance. Jesus tells us, "I say unto you, that likewise joy shall be in heaven over one sinner that repenteth, more than over ninety and nine just persons, which need no repentance" (Luke 15:7). But the effect in the sinner's life is glorious too. Man is to repent "that your sins may be blotted out" (Acts 3:19). These separate from fellowship with God. There is no other way of securing pardon. When a man repents, he receives the gift of the Holy Spirit (Acts 2:38) which brings new life.

III. FAITH IS REQUIRED IN SALVATION
(Hebrews 11:1-6)

The writer of Hebrews defines faith as "the substance of things hoped for, the evidence of things not seen" (11:1). Someone has roughly translated this verse to read, "Faith gives reality to things hoped for." Whatever faith is, it is the other condition besides repentance upon which salvation depends.

There are different kinds of faith, but all faith has the same basis. It has been defined as "belief of testimony." It is the "intellectual instrument with which we lay hold of objects which the mind only can perceive." Whereas knowledge involves observation and experience, faith is reliance on the testimony of someone else.

True faith or the faith of the gospel is belief in the divine testimony. Its difference to common faith is not in its nature but in its circumstances. God has testified and given revelation of things which are beyond the range of human vision. This involves the character of God, the need of man, God's provision of salvation, and the way to Heaven. The faith of the gospel is hearty assent to this revelation of God. It involves the agreement of the heart that it is true and the conviction of the understanding so that man acts upon it. It is simply taking God at His Word.

The *Treatise* statement on saving faith states that it is "an assent of the mind to the fundamental truths of revelation, an acceptance of the Gospel, through the influence of the Holy Spirit, and a firm confidence and trust in Christ. The fruit of faith is obedience to the Gospel." Briefly this makes faith to consist of (1) consent of the mind to the truths of revelation, (2) acceptance of these truths, and (3) a personal confidence and trust in Jesus Christ. Faith is more than just belief, trust, or hope. Probably belief and trust together come as near as anything in giving the best definition of faith.

Saving faith gives such a reality to the invisible truths of God that they have real existence in the mind of the believer. "With the heart man believeth unto righteousness," said Paul. Faith enables the believer to act as if the promises of God were present and seen by his naked eye. The believer's confidence in the reality of the things of God is more satisfactory and conclusive than reason. He acts and feels as if they are true.

Saving faith is a channel which a man opens to let the grace of God flow into his life. Man is "dead in trespasses and sins." God is holy. Thus a great chasm exists, barring fellowship between the two.

But the grace of God can span this gap if man will reach out by faith and accept the provisions of God for restoring fellowship and removing the enmity.

This saving faith is a setting of the heart to proceed upon all the inspirations of the Word and to do all the commandments of the Word. It is to believe God in such a way that one acts in accordance with His Word. A believer should let his affections be governed by the Word of God. He should make all his life's decisions by the Word.

The power to believe is the gift of God. Paul said that it is "not of yourselves: it is the gift of God" (Ephesians 2:8). Jesus is the "author and finisher of our faith" (Hebrews 12:2). The Holy Spirit works in man enabling him to believe in God (Galatians 5:5). But although faith is of God, it is the responsibility of each man, who permits God to create faith in him. As the *Treatise* says, "The power to believe is the gift of God, but believing is an act of the creature."

Faith is a reasonable demand of God before He saves a man. It is only right and just for God who has provided for salvation to require man to believe what He has done. There is no merit in faith. Faith, someone has said, is merely reaching out the hand to receive what God has to offer. So salvation is offered by God. He wants man to accept it. Faith is man's means of appropriating that salvation.

The works which James teaches (2:14-16) are an expression of the faith teaching of Paul (Romans 4:1-12). The *Treatise* says, "The fruit of faith is obedience to the Gospel." The works of faith are not meritorious but are only exhibits of a faith that saves and changes a life. When a person believes, rest, peace, assurance, and joy flood into his life (Romans 5:1; Hebrews 4:1-6; 1 Peter 1:8). The result of these things in a life will be a prompting of the believer to do godly works. Jesus said, "He that believeth on me, the works that I do shall he do also; and greater works than these shall he do; because I go unto my Father" (John 14:12).

IV. REGENERATION IS THE RESULT OF REPENTANCE AND FAITH
(John 3:1-8)

Repentance and faith are the only conditions which God has placed upon man. Both of these are non-meritorious but are necessary conditions. God works in bringing influences to bear upon the sinner to bring him to conviction. Then when these lead the individual to respond in repentance and faith, God begins His work in salvation.

Regeneration is the result of man's response to God. Regeneration, or New Birth as Jesus described it to Nicodemus, is necessary to spiritual living. Man naturally is in a depraved condition. The Word of God describes him as "dead in trespasses and sins" (Ephesians 2:1). This is why Jesus said, "Except a man be born again, he cannot see the kingdom of God'" (John 3:3). A moral change must take place in a man's life before he can enjoy fellowship with God.

This change is regeneration when viewed from God's side. From man's side it is usually called conversion. Man is passive in regeneration. God does the work. In it a new divine life is communicated to the soul of man. As he submits to God in repentance and faith, a new nature is imparted to him. This must never be thought of as a mere change in one's profession from one religion to another. Neither is it wrought by the act of baptism. Regeneration is not reformation, though reformation of the life will surely result.

Regeneration is an internal change wrought in the inner man by the Holy Spirit. It includes (1) a change in the governing purpose of the mind. The former mind was governed by self; the new, by God. (2) It involves a change in one's chief object of affection. Formerly loving the things of the world, the new man in Christ will love the things of God and Christ. (3) There will be a change in one's moral tendencies. Whereas the old man was a slave to sin, the born again person will tend to love holiness and righteousness. Although there will be no outward physical changes in the person, he will be a new creature in Christ.

This change is referred to in the Bible under different figures of speech. It is called "being quickened'" (Ephesians 2:1; Colossians 2:13), passing "from death unto life" (John 5:24; 1 John 3:14), and partaking "of the divine nature'" (2 Peter 1:4; Hebrews 3:14; 6:4).

Two agents of regeneration are mentioned in the Bible. It has already been stated that regeneration is a divine work. This is that of which John wrote when he said that we are "born, not of blood, nor of the will of the flesh, nor of the will of man, but of God" (John 1:13). God "of his own will'" begat us (James 1:18). But the Holy Spirit is the divine agent in regeneration. This is why Jesus spoke to Nicodemus saying, "Except a man be born . . . of the Spirit, he cannot enter into the kingdom of God" (John 3:5), and "that which is born of the Spirit is spirit'" (3:6). Writing to Titus, Paul spoke of the New Birth as a "renewing of the Holy Ghost" (Titus 3:5).

Peter speaks also of the instrumentality of the Word of God in regeneration. In 1 Peter 1:23 he wrote, "Being born again, not of corruptible seed, but of incorruptible, by the word of God, which liveth and abideth for ever'" (see also 1 Corinthians 4:15). However, we must recognize that the Word is not sufficient within itself. If this were true, men would be saved by simply embracing the Word of God brought to them by men. Surely the preaching of the Word is vital and necessary, but the renewing of the heart is the special prerogative of the Holy Spirit (2 Thessalonians 2:13). At the moment of repentance and faith, the Holy Spirit by an instantaneous act brings life to the believer. He becomes a child of God by that new birth (Galatians 3:26).

V. JUSTIFICATION AND SANCTIFICATION ARE BY-PRODUCTS OF REGENERATION
(Romans 5:1-11)

The work of God is not complete in regeneration alone. The Word of God describes other divine transactions which take place at the time of regeneration and following it. Justification and sanctification are also wrought at that time.

Justification is related to regeneration. But regeneration is a work wrought in us while justification is an act of God toward us.

Justification is a word describing the new standing which man has before God as he is declared righteous and acceptable before God. The *Treatise* describes this by saying, "Personal justification implies that the person justified has been guilty before God; and, in consideration of the atonement of Christ, accepted by faith, the sinner is pardoned and absolved from the guilt of sin and restored to the divine favor."

Justification then is a change in man's relation or standing before God. Relations that have been disturbed by sin are corrected. He who had been guilty and condemned is now acquitted and accepted into the fellowship of God. This is a declarative act of God based upon the redemption found in the atoning death of Christ (Romans 3:24-26).

Justification consists of two chief elements: (1) the forgiveness of sin and the removal of its guilt and punishment (Romans 8:1); and (2) the imputation of the righteousness of Christ and restoration to God's favor.

Sanctification is both an act and a process. It is an act of God at the moment of salvation by which the believer is put into a state of dedication unto God and separation from the evil of the world. These are the two chief elements in sanctification (Hebrews 10:10, 14).

As a process, sanctification is a continuing growth of the believer in the grace of God (2 Peter 3:18). Although justification and regeneration are complete, there are privileges and attainments yet to be achieved and enjoyed by every believer. The process which brings the believer to a realization of these is sanctification. A radical change begins the believer's spiritual life, but this commencement is to be followed by many other growth changes. The Bible is full of exhortations to this end. The believer will be engaged in a warfare against sin. He is to fight the good fight of faith, to watch and pray, to grow in grace, and to ever press on. All these are found to be needful to the Christian experience. The renewed soul, though free from condemnation, is susceptible to temptation and prone to yield to influences from the world. It must ever engage in an overcoming life and progress in sanctification.

The Scriptures set forth an ultimate, complete, and final sanctification. Paul described this state when he wrote, "Brethren, I count not myself to have apprehended: but this one thing I do, forgetting those things which are behind, and reaching forth unto those things which are before, I press toward the mark for the prize of the high calling of God in Christ Jesus" (Philippians 3:13, 14). This will be the time when "that which is perfect is come" (1 Corinthians 13:10). It is that goal mentioned by Paul in his prayer to the Thessalonians that "the very God of peace sanctify you wholly" (1 Thessalonians 5:23).

Chapter Six

7

Perseverance of the Saints

BACKGROUND

For centuries Baptists have been divided over the idea of whether a Christian can lose his salvation. Even during the days of the Anabaptists there was the disagreement over this subject; although, it seems that most Anabaptists believed in the possibility of apostasy.

The group of people who formed the Baptist church, which was actually the beginning of the modern Baptist movement, believed it was possible for Christians to be lost.

Later, another church was formed which believed that Christ died for a particular number and called themselves Particular Baptists. They also believed that once a person was saved, he could not lose his salvation.

The older group was called General Baptists to emphasize their belief that the atonement of Christ was general, that is, for all men.

The Particular Baptists accepted John Calvin's five points as opposed to the Arminian theology of the General Baptists.

All Baptists today are either Calvinistic or Arminian. Of course, there are varying degrees of each doctrine, especially among the Calvinists.

In today's lesson the historical stand of Free Will Baptists will be studied. It should prove of great interest to every individual, and it should serve as an incentive to reaffirm one's faith in the principles which identify the Free Will Baptists as a distinctive group of Baptists.

It has been at this very point of doctrine that foes of the denomination have aimed their darts. It would be well that Free Will Baptists be made aware of why the denomination believes in a doctrine which so many people regard as contradictory, for, indeed, God's people are to be "a peculiar people, zealous of good works."

It is just as important today as it was years ago to uphold this particular doctrine of our faith.

OUTLINE

I. The Preservation of the Saints (Roman 8:35-39)
II. The Perseverance of the Saints
    A. The Conditional Nature of Salvation (2 Chronicles 15:1-4)
    B. The Need for Continuance (Ezekiel 33:12-15)
    C. The Possibility of Apostasy (Hebrews 6:4-6)
    D. The Need for Growth (2 Peter 1:1-10)

INTRODUCTION

One of the distinctive doctrines of Free Will Baptists is the doctrine of the perseverance of the saints. The denomination is the largest Baptist group that is not Calvinistic in doctrine. Free Will Baptists are referred to as Arminian in doctrine. After John Calvin established the Reformation church in its doctrines of election, limited atonement, irresistible grace, and perseverance (preservation) of the saints, a man by the name of Jacobus Arminius arose to refute these with his teachings of an unlimited atonement with free grace for all who would believe, and the possibility of making shipwreck of faith. Free Will Baptists were born out of a succession of men who adhered to this faith.

The young denomination was almost destroyed by many of its members and churches going to Calvinism around 1750-60. The Randall Movement, which was the northern branch of the denomination, was almost totally lost to Calvinism in 1911 with the merger with the Northern Baptist Convention.. The remaining churches regrouped, however, and the Free Will Baptist denomination was more "dyed-in-the-wool" Arminian than ever before.

The doctrine which Free Will Baptists oppose will be given first in brief so that our people can better understand our own doctrine.

I. THE PRESERVATION OF THE SAINTS
(Romans 8:35-39)

This doctrine was originally referred to as the perseverance of the saints when used by the Calvinists. This was misleading, however, since the Calvinistic doctrine of election taught that the elect were eternally secure and could not be lost. This doctrine of the necessary persistence of saints in salvation would, therefore, be better captioned as the preservation of the saints since it is of God who preserves and not of saints who persevere.

The extreme of this doctrine has been the teaching which says that because a person in justification is delivered from sin he is eternally safe no matter what he becomes in life and conduct. Many have taught this "once saved, always saved" theory and have indicated that even though a life of sin was pursued, the "justified" person was eternally secure.

Actually, most of those who hold to the doctrine of the preservation of the saints do not go this far. They insist that their doctrine does not teach that a person is saved whether he persists in faith or not, but rather that a believer will persist in faith and will attain final salvation. They teach that the truly regenerated man will persevere and be saved, that God will keep His children and cause them to persevere. God preserves the Christian by causing him to persevere.

Various Scriptures are used to support this view. For example, 1 John 3:6-9 is used to teach that the new life within the believer is imperishable in its nature. This new life guarantees persistence in the fight on sin until sin is conquered. John 14:19 and 1 John 4:4 are used to show that Christ dwells in the believer and is greater than Satan. Because He is in us, we cannot be overcome. Christ who is in us will deliver us in the end from the wrath of God (Romans 5:9, 10).

Calvinists also use the intercession of Christ to support their doctrine. Using Christ's intercession of Peter as an example (Luke 22:31, 32), they seek to demonstrate that Christ kept Peter and he was not lost. Likewise, they believe that He guarded the other disciples and prayed for their continuing protection (John 17:11-15). They say that the son of perdition, Judas, was lost, but he was never saved. "Wherefore he is able also to save them to the uttermost that come unto God by him, seeing he ever liveth to make intercession for them" (Hebrews 7:25) is also used to support this view.

Another point used is the sealing by the Holy Spirit (Ephesians 1:13; 4:30). They say that the Holy Spirit is given by God as a pledge that God will complete our redemption.

Those who follow the "once saved, always saved" theory also take other isolated Scriptures to support their view. One is John 10:28, 29 which they interpret to say that Jesus gives His sheep eternal life and they shall never perish for no one can snatch them out of the Father's hand. John 5:24 is taken to teach that a believer cannot once again come under condemnation.

Probably one of the most used Scriptures to support this doctrine is in Romans 8:35-39. This passage, like the others used by these teachers, contains a precious thought, but not the one given to it. This passage asks the question, "Who shall separate us from the love of Christ?" After listing many things Paul concludes that none of these "shall be able to separate us from the love of God, which is in Christ Jesus our Lord" (verse 39). Surely every believer will agree that nothing can separate us from the love of God. But this passage is not dealing with whether or not a person can be lost after he is saved. It is not an outside power as mentioned here that separates a man from God. It is his own choice. It is making shipwreck of faith. Truly angels, powers, and principalities cannot separate one from the love of God, but a man can of his own choice reject the Spirit of God which has saved him.

Thiessen gives four proofs for his view on perseverance. (1) *The purpose of God.* Supporting this he quotes Isaiah 14:24 where the Lord says, "Surely as I have thought, so shall it come to pass; and as I have purposed, so shall it stand." He also quotes Paul's statement in Romans 8:35-39. He argues that Jesus' statement in John 10:27-30 is unconditional where He says, "My sheep hear my voice, and I know them, and they follow me: And I give unto them eternal life; and they shall never perish, neither shall any man pluck them out of my hand. My Father, which gave them me, is greater than all; and no man is able to pluck them out of my Father's hand. I and my Father are one."

(2) *The Mediatorship of Christ.* This is the continuing intercession of Christ. To support this he quotes Paul who said, "God commendeth his love toward us, in that, while we were yet sinners, Christ died for us. Much more then, being now justified by his blood, we shall be saved from wrath through him. For if, when we were enemies, we were reconciled to God by the death of his Son,

much more, being reconciled, we shall be saved by his life" (Romans 5:8-10). He also quoted from the book of Hebrews where the author wrote, "Wherefore he is able also to save them to the uttermost that come unto God by him, seeing he ever liveth to make intercession for them" (Hebrews 7:25).

(3) *God's Continued Ability to Keep Us.* Thiessen argues that God is not only willing but also able to keep us. He quoted Paul who said, "Being confident of this very thing, that he which hath begun a good work in you will perform it until the day of Jesus Christ" (Philippians 1:6). He also used the words of Peter which speaks of saints "who by the power of God are guarded through faith unto a salvation ready to be revealed in the last time" (1 Peter 1:5, *American Standard Version*).

(4) *The Nature of the Change in the Believer.* In regeneration the believer receives a new life that is eternal. The life imparted is eternal. It is a change in a sphere of the inner life over which man has no control. The Son of God can no more lose His sonship than an earthly son can lose his. He "hath everlasting life" (John 3:36).

Although the opposite view will be presented in the next section of this lesson, let us note these objections to the "once saved, always saved" theory: (1) It induces laxness in conduct and encourages laziness in the Lord's service. (2) It robs man of his freedom if he no longer can control his life. With no power to choose, he is a mere automation or mechanical device. (3) The Scriptures teach contrary to this view. All Scriptures have to be compared rather than just taking isolated passages upon which to base a view as is done by those who adhere to this view. (4) The Bible is full of warnings and exhortations to the saved which would seem unnecessary if the security doctrine were true. Why should the eternally secure be warned if they were in no danger of falling? Let us now turn to a positive study of the doctrine of perseverance.

II. THE PERSEVERANCE OF THE SAINTS
(Romans 8:35-39)

This study is best undertaken by breaking it down into subjects. Let us note each of the headings as they relate to perseverance.

A. The Conditional Nature of Salvation (2 Chronicles 15:1-4)

Free Will Baptists as a denomination teach (1) that salvation is conditional and (2) that the security of believers is conditional. This doctrine stands opposed to the doctrine which teaches that God elects some people to be saved and some to be damned. It also stands in opposition to the doctrine which teaches "once saved, always saved."

The "if-condition" was introduced early in the history of man. It was of Cain, the son of Adam and Eve, that the Lord said, "If thou doest well, shalt thou not be accepted?" And it was Cain who was rejected because he refused to meet the condition; therefore he "went out from the presence of the LORD" (Genesis 4:7, 16).

God said to Abraham, "Walk before me, and be thou perfect. And I will make my covenant between me and thee, and will multiply thee exceedingly" (Genesis 17:1, 2). The fact that there were conditions in this covenant is brought out in several places. In Hebrews 11:8 it is reported that "By faith Abraham, when he was called to go . . . obeyed." Abraham had been told, "Thou shalt keep my covenant therefore, thou, and thy seed after thee in their generations" (Genesis 17:9). Those succeeding generations who did not keep these commandments were cut off.

The covenant of God with Israel was based on conditions. At Sinai when it was instituted, God said, "If ye will obey my voice indeed, and keep my covenant, then ye shall be a peculiar treasure unto me above all people" (Exodus 19:5). Later there were six "ifs" recorded for this covenant: (1) "If ye walk in my statutes, and keep my commandments, and do them." (2) "If ye will not hearken unto me, and will not do all these commandments." (3) "If ye shall despise my statutes, or if your soul abhor my judgments." (4) "If ye will not yet for all this hearken unto me." (5) "If ye walk contrary unto me." (6) "If ye will not be reformed by me by these things" (Leviticus 26:3, 14, 15, 18, 21, 23).

These conditions may be found throughout the remainder of the Old Testament. In every instance of an offer of salvation or blessing, the conditions are either stated or implied. Probably the essential point of the matter was stated by Azariah the prophet to Asa the king in the passage given in the heading of this section. The prophet said to the king, "The LORD is with you, while ye be with him; and if ye seek him, he will be found of you; but if ye forsake him, he will forsake you" (2 Chronicles 15:2). The condition is plainly stated. A proper relation between God and man requires the willingness of both parties. God wants to enter into redemptive relations with man. But God does not impose His will upon unwilling man.

In the New Testament this same principle is followed. Salvation is always conditional. Even in John 3:16 the salvation promised is based upon "whosoever will." Jesus said on another occasion, "Whosoever he be of you that forsaketh not all that he hath, he cannot be my disciple" (Luke 14:33). In John 8:51 Jesus said, "Verily, verily, I say unto you, If a man keep my saying, he shall never see death." To His disciples on another occasion Jesus remarked, "If any man will come after me, let him deny himself, and take up his cross, and follow me" (Matthew 16:24).

Paul, the great apostle of salvation by faith and the doctrines of election, predestination, and adoption, was not silent about conditions in salvation. He tells us that the Jewish branches were broken off "because of unbelief" (Romans 11:20). The Gentiles were enjoying the opportunity and would continue to do so "if thou continue in his goodness: otherwise thou also shalt be cut off" (11:22). Elsewhere to warn believers he wrote, "If ye live after the flesh, ye shall die: but if ye through the Spirit do mortify the deeds of the body, ye shall live" (Romans 8:13).

In John's epistles several references to conditions in salvation are mentioned. In his first letter he wrote, "If that which ye have heard from the beginning shall remain in you, ye also shall continue in the Son, and in the Father" (2:24). He also wrote that "Whosoever transgresseth, and abideth not in the doctrine of Christ, hath not God" (2 John 9).

If the Scriptures make salvation conditional to some men, it must be conditional to all. The majority of the offers of salvation have a definitely stated condition. In the New Testament repentance and faith are stated as conditions of entering into salvation. Continuance in faith is then stated or implied as the condition of continuing in salvation. Although works are never implied or stated to be a condition, the Scriptures plainly state that faith will result in works, faith will be demonstrated by words, and a faith without works is dead. Salvation is conditioned upon a growth in grace, for after listing Christian graces to be assumed by the believer, Peter wrote, "If ye do these things, you shall never fall" (2 Peter 1:10). So, salvation is a dynamic thing in a life.

B. The Need for Continuance (Ezekiel 33:12-15)

The conditional nature of salvation and the believer's security makes continuance in the development of faith and conduct a necessity. The *Free Will Baptist Articles of Faith* (pages 43, 44 of the *Treatise*) state the terms of salvation to be not only faith and repentance but also "continuance in faith and obedience until death." In these same articles in the one defining perseverance, the statement is made that "All believers in Christ, who through grace persevere in holiness to the end of life, have promise of eternal salvation." These statements are based upon definite scriptural assertions.

In this passage from Ezekiel, an oft repeated biblical principle is briefly stated by this prophet, "The righteousness of the righteous shall not deliver him in the day of this transgression" (33:12). The prophet is apparently saying that when a godly man discontinues the godly way of life and by transgression deliberately leaves that godly pattern of living, he can no longer claim the blessings of his relationship to God.

This is further substantiated in the next verse where the prophet continued by saying, "When I shall say to the righteous, that he shall surely live; if he trust to his own righteousness, and commit iniquity, all his righteousness shall not be remembered; but for his iniquity that he hath committed, he shall die for it" (verse 13). The prophet speaking for God taught that a righteous man could not forsake the godly way of life without losing the benefits of life in God. If he committed transgression (a deliberate breaching of the known law of God) or iniquity (a life of perversion), his past relations to God were severed.

Jesus stated this same principle of continuance in the New Testament. On one occasion He said, "He that endureth to the end shall be saved" (Matthew 10:22). Jesus was talking about the believers living under extreme persecution. Surely He was not talking about physical salvation from persecution. This is not always promised. He apparently was talking about continuance in the Christian life to the end even though it had to be maintained through the severest trials.

Paul had a similar principle in mind when he wrote to the Galatians saying, "And let us not be weary in well doing: for in due season we shall reap, if we faint not" (6:9). In his letter to the Ephesians he had barely written that our salvation is "not of works" (2:9) when he immediately said, "We are his workmanship, created in Christ Jesus unto good works, which God hath before ordained that we should walk in them" (verse 10). Surely the implication is that the believer's continuance in the faith is evidenced by the type of life he lives.

John the Revelator, writing to the seven churches of Asia, had continuance in the Christian experience as a central thought in his message. The message of Christ to the church at Laodicea is probably typical of what John wrote to each. To them it was written, "To him that overcometh will I grant to sit with me in my throne" (Revelation 3:21). To the church at Thyatira he had written, "He that overcometh, and keepeth my works unto the end, to him will I give power over the nations" (2:26).

What has been said was not intended to infer that the believer's continuance in the faith depends solely on the believer. We need to recognize that only by the help of God is a believer enabled to continue in the faith. Our *Treatise* states that "There are strong grounds to hope that the truly regenerate will persevere unto the end, and be saved, through the power of divine grace which is pledged for their support." Without this divine grace the believer would have no power for continuance. All his strength to persevere comes from the grace of God.

C. The Possibility of Apostasy (Hebrews 6:4-6)

The doctrine most vitally related to perseverance is the question of the possibility of apostasy. If apostasy is not possible or stated in the Word of God, then the doctrine of the preservation of the saints is unquestionably correct. Free Will Baptists believe the Scriptures do teach that in regard to believers "their future obedience and final salvation are neither determined nor certain, since through infirmity and manifold temptations they are in danger of falling; and they ought, therefore, to watch and pray lest they make shipwreck of their faith and be lost."

Although far from being the only one, the passage in Hebrews 6:4-6 is probably the best statement and most conclusive of any in the New Testament. Surely a saved person is described in the words, "once enlightened, and have tasted of the heavenly gift, and were made partakers of the Holy Ghost and have tasted the good word of God, and the powers of the world to come" (6:4, 5). If one of such an experience is not saved, it is hard to imagine what it would take to describe a true believer. Even many securitists admit that a saved person is described but try to diminish the meaning of the passage by interpreting the full passage as a hypothetical situation that will never take place. However, the Scripture plainly states that "it is impossible . . . if they shall fall away, to renew them again unto repentance (6:4, 6). The passage surely describes a possibility and a condition that cannot be remedied.

If the believer could not be lost after he was saved, Paul's writings would appear absurd. He warned each Corinthian believer to "take heed lest he fall" (1 Corinthians 10:12). He told Timothy that "some shall depart from the faith" (1 Timothy 4:1) and mentions those who are "reprobate concerning the faith" (2 Timothy 3:8). This term *reprobate* is used of those who have abandoned the faith in 2 Corinthians 13:6, 7. Paul suggested to Titus that an apostate was one who was "subverted" and "sinneth" and therefore "condemned" (Titus 3:11).

In the beautiful analogy of Jesus regarding the vine and the branches, Jesus seems to make the possibility of apostasy evident. His only picture is of believers in a proper relation to Him. But He said, "If a man abide not in me [the Greek would allow, "If a man does not continue to abide in me"],' he is cast forth as a branch, and is withered; and men gather them, and cast them into the fire, and they are burned" (John 15:6). Jesus was probably describing the apostate when He spoke of the "blasphemy against the Holy Ghost," which He said would "not be forgiven unto men" (Matthew 12:31).

Peter makes several mentions of the apostate. He describes them as "servants of corruption: for of whom a man is overcome, of the same is he brought in bondage" (2 Peter 2:19). He went on to say, "For if after they have escaped the pollutions of the world through the knowledge of the Lord and Saviour Jesus Christ, they are again entangled therein, and overcome, the latter end is worse with them than the beginning" (verse 20). That Peter was describing a saved person is explicit from the following facts: (1) These persons had escaped the pollutions of the world. (2) From the state they were in they had to be overcome to return to a former condition. (3) They had a knowledge of the Lord and Savior Jesus Christ. (4) They turned from a holy commandment delivered unto them.

The book of Jude is devoted wholly to a description of apostates who "ran greedily after the error of Balaam for reward" (verse 11). These are "twice dead" persons "whose fruit withereth" (verse 12). The believers to whom Jude wrote were urged to "Keep yourselves in the love of God" (verse 21). Jude gives praise to "him that is able to keep you from falling" (verse 24). How absurd such a prayer is if falling is impossible.

The Bible is full of exhortations and warnings addressed to believers. These presuppose the ability to fall away from the grace of God and to be lost. In 1 Chronicles 28:9 we read, "If thou forsake him, he will cast thee off for ever." These words to Solomon are just an example of these warnings which if they refer to an impossible situation make the Word of God seem absurd. But the Word is plain in other places that these do not describe impossibilities. Even angels, we are told, "kept not their first estate, but left their own habitation" (Jude 6). In the story of the rich man and Lazarus, we find the rich man, a son of the Abrahamic family, in Hell. If the covenants of God are without condition, how did this happen? Likewise, Paul uses the Jews as a nation who were cut off. And why were they cut off? Paul said, "Because of unbelief they were broken off" (Romans 11:20). To Gentiles who had believed, he then wrote, "For if God spared not the natural branches, take heed lest he also spare not thee" (verse 21). Thus the evidence piles up

as one searches the Scriptures to show that a believer is a participant with God in his own salvation. This is why it is expedient for
each to "work out your own salvation with fear and trembling"
(Philippians 2:12).

D. The Need for Growth (2 Peter 1:1-10)

Because of the possibility of falling, every believer should give
himself to growth in grace so that he will be able to overcome.
Peter's total message in the book of Second Peter seems to be to
encourage believers to deepen their experience (knowledge) of the
one who saved them (1:2). Grace is the unmerited favor of God.
Peace is that condition which results from a right relationship. To
achieve this growth, he lays out a formula by which they are to
live. This is by adding to the faith by which they were saved (1:5).

Peter predicts two things for believers: (1) "If these things be in
you, and abound" (verse 8), if there is a continual growth in the
believer, he will not "be barren nor unfruitful in the knowledge
of our Lord Jesus Christ." (2) The person who lacks growth in his
life will become "blind" and will forget "that he was purged from
his old sins" (verse 9). The believer is urged not to let this latter
happen to him but to "give diligence to make your calling and
election sure: for if ye do these things, ye shall never fall" (verse 10).
He concludes his book with a warning, "Beware lest ye . . . fall from
your own stedfastness. But grow in grace, and in the knowledge of
our Lord and Saviour Jesus Christ" (3:17, 18).

The great burden of Paul's epistles is the growth of believers. In
First and Second Corinthians he deals with problems of believers
which threaten their spiritual lives. To them he wrote: "Examine
yourselves, whether ye be in the faith; prove your own selves.
Know ye not your own selves, how that Jesus Christ is in you?" (2
Corinthians 13:5). In Ephesians he urges them to live a life
"Proving what is acceptable unto the Lord" (5:10). He urges the
believer to "be strong in the Lord, and in the power of his might"

(6:10) and to "Put on the whole armour of God" (verse 11). He urged the Colossian believers to "walk worthy of the Lord unto all pleasing, being fruitful in every good work, and increasing in the knowledge of God; strengthened with all might, according to his glorious power, unto all patience and longsuffering" (Colossians 1:10, 11).

This growth is our sanctification. The *Treatise* says, "Sanctification is the continuing of God's grace by which the Christian may constantly grow in grace and in the knowledge of our Lord Jesus Christ." There are privileges and attainments which no believer ever attains or enjoys. Most live beneath the potential they have in Christ. Each of us like Paul should be able to say, "I count not myself to have apprehended: but this one thing I do, forgetting those things which are behind, and reaching forth unto those things which are before, I press toward the mark for the prize of the high calling of God in Christ Jesus" (Philippians 3:13, 14). Such a goal will insure one's perseverance in the faith and will bring an enriched experience.

Chapter Seven

8

The Church and THE Church

BACKGROUND

Various definitions of the church have been given by many who were influenced by their own particular theology. The Roman Catholics have declared that the Roman Catholic Church is the only church and that salvation is in it. The term *catholic* indicates this belief for it means general or universal.

Many Protestants have attempted to avoid the idea of succession directly to the apostles by regarding the church in a twofold manner: a visible church and an invisible church. A number of these men have applied the term *church* to a denomination which is a false application.

Besides the denomination idea, other definitions have been proposed. Some speak of the building as the church. The Bible knows no such definition.

There are many Baptists who hold to the idea that the Bible definition of the word *church* is a congregation of believers who have covenanted together to meet at stated times to worship God, who believe and practice those things taught by Christ and His apostles, and who keep the ordinances. This definition, of course, refers to the local church, and the majority of times the word is mentioned in the Bible it is the local church to which it refers. Even the times that some would say refer to the church in a general way are thought by some to be futuristic, or at least could be interpreted as referring to the local congregation.

The idea of succession is held by some to refer to the main principles of the group rather than a historical succession. A church is identified by its faith and practices rather than by its name. A church practicing and teaching the faith practiced and taught by the apostles would be a church of God, regardless of its origin.

Briefly, these are some ideas regarding the church. Regardless of how one believes, however, the main thing is to be right with God and then to follow the teachings in God's Word as closely as possible.

OUTLINE

I. **The Basis of a Christian Church (Matthew 16:13-20)**
II. **The Body of the Church (Romans 12:1-15; 1 Corinthians 12:12-31)**
III. **The Head of the Church (Colossians 1:18-23)**

INTRODUCTION

The "church" as the world views it overall is coming under heavy attacks from many sources. Of course the church has always sustained heavy attacks in all ages. But these renewed assaults appear to be somewhat different. It is being accused as an ineffective means of meeting the world's problems. All of these accusations are rising as churchmen have begun to participate in the social concerns of the world. Accompanying all of this has been a decisive widening of the breach between those who preach the social gospel and those who stress the redemptive mission of the church. Doctrines of various groups are being adjusted to line up with whatever particular emphasis a church group supports.

In view of all the radical changes being made and the charges of the world being flung at the church, it behooves us to be well acquainted with the constitution of the church and its nature. It needs to be answered whether or not our church must adapt itself to the changing scene and altering concepts being thrust upon world opinion today. It is evident that the majority of denominations are going to conform. Shall Free Will Baptists merely conform for the sake of conformity, or shall we as a denomination seek to be different? The answer lies in the Word of God. Free Will Baptists should search diligently for the scriptural concept of the church and conform as nearly as possible to that concept.

I. THE BASIS OF A CHRISTIAN CHURCH
(Matthew 16:13-20)

The word *church* is used only one time by Jesus in reference to the body of believers who would put their faith in Him. He did use it on one other occasion to refer to the Jewish assembly or court in the matter of settling disputes between men (Matthew 18:17). The word used by Jesus has its background in the concept of the Assembly of Israel. Both the Hebrew and the Greek words refer to "called out ones." The Hebrew word is used for the act of calling and for the assembly of the ones called out. Some have falsely associated the origin of the church with Israel because the word *Assembly* is translated as church in Acts 7:38. Israel was called an assembly or church or "called out ones" because as a nation they were called out from among the others to be a holy nation.

The title of the book of Ecclesiastes is sometimes called "the Preacher." The word *ecclesiastes* is from the same word as church or assembly (*ekklesia*). But the word used for the title of that book would refer to "the one who called the congregation together."

113

It is in the New Testament that the real meaning and idea of the church is derived as we use it. It is a New Testament institution, and the concept of the church should not be lost as the kingdom and Christendom are related to it. It was the church with which Christ so positively identified Himself. Paul tells us that Christ "loved the church, and gave himself for it" (Ephesians 5:25). Paul gave his life extending the influence of the church and confessed that his greatest sin was in persecuting "the church of God" (1 Corinthians 15:9). The church exists for "the perfecting of the saints, for the work of the ministry, for the edifying of the body of Christ" (Ephesians 4:12). It will be complete and will have served its purpose when this is accomplished.

The words of Jesus in saying that He will build His church do not give us too many thoughts about the basic makeup of the church, but it does tell us a lot about the basis for it. In the situation pictured in Matthew 16:13-20, the Lord went to great extent to draw out from the disciples a good, firm confession of who He was. It was Peter, the usual spokesman for the group, who uttered the words which He wanted the group to confess. His words were: "Thou art the Christ, the Son of the living God" (verse 16).

It was this confession to which Jesus was referring when He said, "Upon this rock I will build my church" (verse 18). The Catholics erroneously interpret that Peter (stone) was the rock upon which the church was built. The foundation of the church is Jesus Christ or the profession that Christ is the Son of the living God. Only those who make such a profession are eligible for membership in the church of Jesus Christ.

This profession which serves as the basis of the church does not come to men naturally. Only those who have spiritual insight can make such a confession. Jesus said to Peter, "Flesh and blood hath not revealed it unto thee, but my Father which is in heaven" (verse 17). This reminds us of the later words of John who said, "He that hath the Son hath life; and he that hath not the Son of God hath not life" (1 John 5:12). He also wrote: "Whosoever denieth the Son, the same hath not the Father" (1 John 2:23).

This event in the life of Christ and the disciples brings to us the first mention of the church in the New Testament. It might be said that the words of Christ recorded here contain a picture of the church in prophecy and in promise. Jesus had now brought a group of men together who would profess, "Thou art the Christ, the Son of the living God." Upon this confession He both promised and predicted, "I will build my church."

Historically, the beginning of the church must be traced to the first two chapters of Acts and the day of Pentecost which followed the ascension of Christ. These two chapters give us the first account of the Christian Church. Herein is described its glorious beginning. Although predicted previously, it now had a concrete existence in Jerusalem. It was constituted by those who believed in Jesus Christ and through their relation to Him had been regenerated. Luke writes, "And the Lord added to the church daily such as should be saved" (Acts 2:47).

Membership in the church involves conditions related to the very basis of the church. (1) Repentance and baptism are required of all who become members of His church. At Pentecost Peter told those inquiring what to do to become part of this group: "Repent, and be baptized every one of you in the name of Jesus Christ for the remission of sins, and ye shall receive the gift of the Holy Ghost" (Acts 2:38). (2) Another requirement or condition is faith in the Lord Jesus Christ as the divine Redeemer. To the Philippian jailer, inquiring of the way of salvation, Paul said, "Believe on the Lord Jesus Christ, and thou shalt be saved, and thy house" (Acts 16:31). All of Peter's sermon at Pentecost stresses this great fact—turn in faith to Christ. (3) When men meet these two conditions, God takes care of the other in that He saves or regenerates the responding soul: "The Lord added to the church daily such as should be saved" (Acts 2:47). There is no other way into the church

except as an act of God. Regeneration qualifies one for membership. Since regeneration is the New Birth, it might be said that
one is born into the church (spiritually not physically).

Following the meeting of these conditions of membership,
other things will result in members' lives. Just as those early members "continued stedfastly in the apostles' doctrine and fellowship"
(Acts 2:42), so members today will seek to adhere to the teachings
of the Word of God. Besides baptism as an open confession of
one's conversion experience, the believer will constantly be confessing Christ as Savior and His power to save men.

The church is set forth under various figures in the New
Testament. It is never viewed as an organization but always as an
organism. The church is often viewed as a body. Two specific ideas
are contained in this symbol: (1) the relation of the church to
Christ who is its head, and (2) the relation of individual members
to each other.

The books written to the Colossians and the Ephesians especially use the symbol of the church as a body. In Ephesians the
church is viewed as the body of Christ; in Colossians Christ is
emphasized as the head of the church. But these figures are used
elsewhere as well. Paul makes much use of this figure in his other
epistles. Paul's greater emphasis in his other epistles is rather on
the relation of members to each other in that body.

The church is also viewed under other symbols. It is viewed as
a temple (Ephesians 2:21), a building (1 Corinthians 3:9), a house
or habitation (1 Timothy 3:15), or a dwelling for the Holy Spirit
(1 Peter 2:5; 1 Corinthians 3:16). Possibly a more prominent symbol than these is the portrait of the church as the bride of Christ.
This is used both by Paul (2 Corinthians 11:2; Ephesians 5:22-27)
and John (Revelation 19:7; 22:17; 21:2).

The concept of the church includes different things. Usually in
the New Testament the word applies to a local body of believers.
The ordinary import of the term is this. The apostles organized

churches and used the term generally in this sense (Acts 9:31; 15:41; Romans 16:16; Galatians 1:2; Colossians 4:15).

The *Free Will Baptist Treatise* gives a definition of a Christian church as "an organized body of believers in Christ, who statedly assemble to worship God, and who sustain the ordinances of the Gospel according to the Scriptures." It goes on further to say, "The Church of God, or members of the body of Christ, is the whole body of Christians throughout the whole world, and none but the regenerate are its members."

This statement adds another definition of the church for us. Besides the local church there is then a universal church. These two are sometimes distinguished as local and universal or as visible and invisible. The universal church is not a visible organization of believers but is composed of all those who have become children of God by faith in Jesus Christ and are united with Him spiritually as their Head. It was this universal church of which Jesus spoke when He said, "Upon this rock I will build my church" (Matthew 16:18). It is this concept of the church which Paul describes in Ephesians as the body of Christ.

The terms *visible* and *local* do not refer to the same concept. By visible church reference is made to all people who are members of church organizations throughout the world. The term local church refers to any local organized body of believers. This local church would be a part of the visible church. These stand in contrast to the invisible church which consists not of people who can't be seen, but of people of all ages who have become linked together and to Christ through an "invisible," spiritual relation. The visible church is of a mixed nature. Only the regenerate are members of the invisible church.

A word about terminology might be added. Our denomination should not be referred to as the Free Will Baptist Church. Only local churches should be referred to in this manner, such as "the Free Will Baptist Church in a certain city." When a particular group of churches refer to their denomination such as the Methodist Church, or the Catholic Church, or the Church of Christ, it should always be kept in mind that no particular group has an exclusive right to be the church.

II. THE BODY OF THE CHURCH
(Romans 12:1-15; 1 Corinthians 12:12-31)

Paul uses a very elaborate form of speech in 1 Corinthians 12 to describe the body of Christ—the church. It is a human body that Paul uses as the object lesson to describe the church. Even though Paul had been showing that individuals receive gifts from the Spirit, in this section of materials he demonstrates that it is the body of Christ, the church as a whole, that receives those gifts.

A body is one, but it has many members. The members, being many, form one body. A body is an organism that can be one only if it possesses all those members which constitute it. In an organism all the members are governed from one center and it has one life which issues from one source. After describing such a body, Paul adds, "So also is Christ" (verse 12). Christ is one body which has many members.

This concept cannot be applied to Christ personally. "Christ" here is referring to that body of which Christ is the head. This idea is consistent with verse 27 of this same chapter and with Paul's teachings elsewhere (Ephesians 1:22, 23). Actually what Paul is seeking to demonstrate is the presence of diversity and yet unity among those who make up the body of Christ. There is a diversity because of varying gifts, but there is unity because of the close union between Christ and believers.

In verse 13 Paul adds a second reason why the church manifests both unity and diversity and why the figure of a body is an appropriate way to describe the church. This reason is found as a consequence in the way in which the church manifests itself. The "we all" represents the diversity. Individual members were once Jews or Gentiles, some slave and some free men. The same diversities continued to exist after they became one body by baptism. By the baptism accomplished by the Holy Spirit (not water baptism) they became one body, the church. Water baptism was not the activity that incorporated them into the one body but an act "by one Spirit," that is the Holy Spirit. It is amazing how people entirely different can find unity in one body. This was especially remarkable in the early church.

As a matter of note, this might be added. The ecumenical spirit which so pervades the world today and is seeking to bring the church into one organization might study this and realize that the true church already possesses ecumenicity. The church is one body today. True ecumenicity is not in an organizational structure, but in the unity wrought by the Spirit of God: "We have been all made to drink into one Spirit." This results in the closest of communion.

Verses 14-16 discuss the existence of a difference which could arise among individual members. Although the figure is of a body, the same figure can apply to the church. Members sometimes do not appreciate the unity of the body, but it is a unity which cannot be abolished. Believers are always related to the body and cannot act effectively apart from recognition of this interrelatedness.

In the next verse (17) Paul shows how sad a condition would result "if the whole body" were only one member. Although it would surely do away with diversity, many functions could not be performed. But this is not true as Paul points out in verses 18, 19. God created the body in such a way that it does have members. Each member has its own special place in the body, and this function is what makes it a part of the body. The body is something more than the totality of its members. Because of its parts and their functions being performed in unity, the lively organism exists.

Paul restates his original thesis in verse 20: There is one body; it has many members. Then from this premise he draws several lessons: (1) If the body is a unity, the members are related because they are members of one organism (verse 21). (2) All members must perform their tasks and no member is unnecessary (verse 22). (3) Appearances are deceptive and what seems to be the feeblest or most unnecessary members are also vital to the total function of the body (verses 22, 23). (4) The order of importance in the body of Christ is ordered by God and intended by Him (verse 24, compare verses 11 and 18).

The perfect balance in the body, or the fact that it is like it is, arises from the plan of God (verse 24). But even though God so disposes to set some members in a place to work where they are unseen and unrecognized, yet they are also indispensable for the working of the body. If these should not perform their task, it would hinder the performance of other members (verse 25). This close relation within the body results in one of two things: (1) If one member suffers, all the rest of the body suffers also, (2) If one member is honored the whole body is honored with it (verse 26).

Although Paul has the local congregation in mind in verse 27, what is said of the local church could apply to the universal church. Paul says that the Corinthian church is a body of Christ. It is an organism formed by Christ and maintained by Him. It has the complete character of a body as described by Paul. In these verses (28-30) Paul shows the diversity of the offices and gifts within the body which he has described.

Speaking in tongues had become a problem in the Corinthian church. Paul is showing them that this is not the only gift and what its actual place is in the church. The offices and gifts in the church and their positions of importance are listed by Paul in this order: (1) Apostles, men directly called by God. (2) Prophets, who like the apostles were to perform only in the first period of the church, are listed second. This office was not as important and universal as that of apostles, but was not restricted to a local area. (3) Teachers were the officers of the local church who taught and preached revelation which had been received. (4) The workers of miracles were those among the prophets who had special powers during the New Testament era. (5) The gifts of healings were nothing comparable to "divine healers" of today. These were gifts in particular situations and not a vocation followed by men. (6) The helps and governments refer to other local offices within the church which aided the body in the accomplishment of its tasks. (7) Only after listing all of these does Paul come to "kinds of tongues." The *glossalalia* or speaking in tongues (the word *unknown* does not appear in the original text), which was so highly regarded by the Corinthians, is listed in place of least esteem by Paul.

The book of Romans adds to our concept of the body of Christ. In Romans 12:1-3 Paul admonishes each believer in the presentation of his body to Christ. Then he discusses the same unity and diversity which Paul has stressed in the Corinthian passage (Romans 12:4, 5). Then he gives an exhortation to the members of the body to perform the particular calling which has been given to them (verses 6-8).

Starting with verse 9 Paul gives some maxims to direct the individual members of the body of Christ in their social relations with other members of the body. Verse 9 itself is a statement of the central principle of Paul's social ethics. Love is set forth as this principle and each of the following maxims is a development of that concept. Love represents the redemptive goodness of God exhibited toward the undeserving (Romans 5:8). A believer through his religious experience comes to know the love of God, and then that love becomes an indwelling energy in him (Romans 5:5). As such it is the source of patience, gentleness, and other characteristic Christian virtues as described in verses 9-21.

The vocation or calling of the body of Christ involves several things: (1) It is to worship God and glorify Him on the earth. In Ephesians 1:4-6, Paul wrote that "He hath chosen us in him before the foundation of the world . . . To the praise of the glory of his grace, wherein he hath made us accepted in the beloved." (2) The body of Christ is to evangelize the world. The Great Commission states this command (Matthew 28:19, 20). The whole book of Acts sees the church launching forth in this activity. (3) The church is to labor to develop each individual believer until he attains the fullness of the stature of Christ. This is the purpose of the gifts given to the members of the body of Christ. Paul discusses this in Ephesians 4:11-15. According to him the gifts were distributed "For the perfecting of the saints, for the work of the ministry, for the edifying of the body of Christ: Till we all come in the unity of the faith, and of the knowledge of the Son of God, unto a perfect man, unto the measure of the stature of the fulness of Christ: That we henceforth be no more children, tossed to and fro" (verses 12-14).

(4) The members of the body of Christ should be constant witnesses for Christ. Jesus said, "Ye shall be witnesses" (Acts 1:8). This should be a normal result of regeneration. The changed life and the joyous testimony should be natural for every believer. (5) The body of Christ is called to share in the future glory of Christ. The church is to be transported some day to the heavenlies (Ephesians 3:10, 21) to enjoy His eternal glory. The body of Christ in anticipation of that glorious day is referred to as the bride of Christ (Revelation 21:2).

III. THE HEAD OF THE CHURCH
(Colossians 1:18-23)

Paul makes a distinctive contribution to Christianity in his picture of Christ as the head of the church. He viewed Christ and His people together as a living unit. He presents Christ to us as the head of a body. As the head, He exercises control and gives direction. Believers are His body. Individually they make up His limbs and organs. Under His direction, they obey His direction and perform His work. The resurrected Christ shares His risen life with them and is the source of their life. This figure of Paul is an excellent means of conveying to us the relation which exists between Christ and the church.

In the background of the passage of Scripture given for this study (Colossians 1:18-23), Paul presents Him who is the head of the church in a twofold significance (verses 15-17). He presented Him first as the pre-existent Lord of Creation, and then in His relation to Creation as (1) the image of God, (2) the Firstborn of every creature, (3) the Creator of all things, and (4) the Sustainer of all things. This Christ who came to earth as a man and died and rose again was before all creation and is the key to creation.

Paul gave this background and relation of Christ to Creation to set a basis for presenting Him as the one who accomplished the divine work of redemption. His relation to the created universe sets a basis for His presentation in relation to our redemption.

In First Corinthians 12:12-31 and in Romans 12:4-21 Paul uses the picture of the body of Christ to show the mutual relations of church members and their obligations. In Ephesians and Colossians Paul uses the figure to show the relation of the body, the church, to Christ as the head of the body. It is this figure which helps us understand Paul's concept of the believers as being "in Christ" and Christ in them (Galatians 3:27, 28).

The church as the body of Christ is not an extension of His incarnation as interpreted in liberal circles. Neither is it to be understood as His "mystical body" in any sense. Paul intended the figure to show the church as the body of Christ for certain well-defined purposes. It was to bring out the concept of the vital relation between Christ and the church, and it does it better than any of the other figures such as a building and its foundation or the husband and wife.

So this figure is to portray the church as being vitalized by the abiding presence of Christ and His risen life in it. It is energized through Him and is the instrument through which He carries on His work.

As the risen head of the church, Christ is given certain titles by Paul: "the beginning, the firstborn from the dead" (verse 18). He is this because His resurrection marked His triumph over all which held man in bondage (Hebrews 2:14, 15). He represented new hope for mankind, and is "the firstfruits of them that slept" (1 Corinthians 15:20, 23). His resurrection is just a token of the resurrection of His people. That resurrection of Christ is participated in by all who share in His resurrection.

Christ who had the same importance in Creation and in Resurrection finds the fulfillment of the divine purpose in this. For it is the Father's will "that in all things he might have the preeminence." In the old creation, He was preeminent. Because of His resurrection life as Head of the church and His impartation of that life to the church, He is preeminent in the new creation as well.

The following verses picture Christ in two positions as a result of His position as head of the church. For one thing He is the reconciler of all things. Paul says that "It pleased the Father that in him should all fulness dwell . . . And . . . by him to reconcile all things unto himself" (verses 19, 20). The Greeks believed there was a succession of divine agencies between God and man under whose control man lived and through whom man had to communicate with God. Paul was fighting this view with his direct teaching that the fullness or totality of the divine essence and power had taken up its residence in Christ. Jesus Christ was the sole mediator between God and the whole of mankind. Displayed in Christ were all the attributes and activities of God—His Spirit, His Word, His wisdom and glory.

It was God's good pleasure to reconcile all things to Himself through Christ, and Christ accomplished this peacemaking through the shedding of His blood on the Cross (Romans 5:1 ff.). The death of Christ was the deed which availed to make man right with God. All things even included sinful men who were unwilling to submit to His will (Philippians 2:11).

But the central purpose of Christ's peacemaking work brings us to His second position—He is the reconciler of His people to God. Paul said, "You, that were sometime alienated and enemies in your mind by wicked works, yet now hath he reconciled in the body of his flesh through death" (verses 21-23). The central purpose of the death of Christ is seen in its bearing upon those who hear the message of reconciliation and who in willing submission gratefully accept the peace with God. "Alienated and enemies," rebels in revolt against God and His authority, these estranged ones are brought to peace with God. A great change is wrought in them because they who were at war with God are now made to be at peace with Him.

But the marvel of it all is that all those who come to be at peace with God are united in a body and He who reconciled them is made their head. The members of that body are then given the ministry of reconciling others through the preaching of the good news of salvation.

Chapter Eight

9

Stewardship of the Believer

BACKGROUND

Tithing has been practiced by people other than Jews and Christians. In the British Museum there are tablets which are receipts for tithes to the temple of the sun god during the time of Nebuchadnezzar.

Knowing that heathen believed in and practiced tithing should put to shame any Christian who refuses to tithe. Can it be said that heathen people love their gods more than Christians do theirs? The main problem is showing the Christian that tithing is scriptural. Many good people have not been convinced that it is scriptural. Once convinced, they will tithe.

There is a need to avoid the error of legalism regarding tithing. Some people teach that tithing is a requirement for salvation. But tithing is no more essential for salvation than any other work. "Not by works of righteousness which we have done, but according to his mercy he saved us" (Titus 3:5a). Tithing is a result, not a condition of salvation.

OUTLINE

I. Stewardship of Life (Matthew 23:16-23)
II. The Old Testament Teaches Tithing (Genesis 14:17-24; 28:12-22; Deuteronomy 24:27-29; Malachi 3:7-15)
III. The New Testament Teaches Tithing (2 Corinthians 9:1-12; 1 Corinthians 16:1, 2)
IV. Tithing Is God's Financial Plan for the Support of His Work (1 Corinthians 9:1-18)

INTRODUCTION

What is Christian stewardship? This question should be one to which every believer constantly gives his effort to find the answer. There are certain basics of Christian stewardship which will hold true in every believer's life, although the Holy Spirit may lead to a different administration in each individual life. Christian stewardship is a broad theme but includes "the practice of systematic and proportionate giving of time, abilities and material possessions, based on the conviction that these are a trust from God, to be used in His service for the benefit of mankind."

Christian stewardship is the recognition of and fulfilment of personal privilege and responsibility for the whole of life in accordance with the spirit and ideals of Christ. This involves personality, time, talent, influence, material substance—everything. So stewardship is the dedication to God of all of our life. Ambitions, loyalties, and vocation are all included. A believer needs to dedicate all of his home life: marriage, children, work, and recreation. He needs to dedicate all of his income and expenditures—family budget, investments, and a definite portion for the church in its worldwide ministry. The believer, too, needs to dedicate all of life's experiences: honors, rewards, failures, triumphs, and heartaches. Stewardship is the dedication of all our heart, mind, will, and strength to God with the recognition that things neither present nor yet to come can separate us from His love. This giving to God must not be just now and then, but regular, systematic, and sacrificial. Otherwise, it is but mockery to God.

I. STEWARDSHIP OF LIFE
(Matthew 23:16-23)

The stewardship of life was expressed by Jesus as He talked with the meticulous scribes and Pharisees. They were so careful to find out exactly what God required of them and to be overly sensitive about meeting the most minute requirements. To them Jesus said, "Woe unto you, scribes and Pharisees, hypocrites! for ye pay tithe of mint and anise and cummin, and have omitted the weightier matters of the law, judgment, mercy, and faith: these ought ye to have done, and not to leave the other undone" (Matthew 23:23). Truly Jesus lent His support to tithing here, but more than that He encouraged stewardship in all areas of life.

The comment of Jesus to these hypocritical religious leaders should encourage every believer to do the following:

1. He should assume the responsibility of carefully analyzing his Christian heritage. What does he possess? Of our time, talents, and possessions we should acknowledge their origin by becoming accountable for their use.

2. He should seek to discover the secret of the most effective use of every gift given to him by the gracious Creator. Before his short day is done and gifts are lost through misuse or nonuse, he should use them for some good accomplishment.

3. The believer should develop an ability to turn to good account every potential which he has. It is so easy to let moments slip, possessions to be used selfishly, or talents to disintegrate from lack of use.

A true sense of vocation and of stewardship go hand in hand. The word *vocation* comes from a Latin word which gives us the

English word *calling*. A man's work should be in answer to a call from God whether he be a layman or clergyman. The call is best obeyed and the answer most completely given when the call is an expression of the natural talents of a person. God's call is always in keeping with one's potential in Him. There may be an inequality of human endowments, but God gives us responsibility equal to the potential given. The following facts should be noted in regard to stewardship of life:

1. Each person is endowed with at least one talent. No person is empty-handed. Sometimes the use of the one talent will bless the world more than the five talents of a more greatly endowed man.

2. The Scriptures teach us that talents unused are soon lost. As an unused muscle loses its power and an unplanted seed its vitality, so an ability unused will disappear.

3. The church has use for a diversity of talents. Many important tasks go undone for lack of dedication of talents. All talents are needed to perform all the functions of the body of Christ.

4. The love of Christ will constrain the believer to become a good steward for God. He has given us so much and we are legally required to do nothing in return. But our love for Him should force us to dedicate our all to Christ.

The biblical ideal of stewardship involves five things which will be discussed in the following paragraphs.

1. By right of creation and redemption God is the one and only Owner of all things which we possess. Abraham acknowledged God to be "the possessor of heaven and earth" (Genesis 14:22). God's claim upon Israel was based upon this statement of Moses: "Behold, the heaven and the heaven of heavens is the LORD's thy God, the earth also, with all that therein is" (Deuteronomy 10:14). Paul taught believers that through redemption they belonged to God. He said, "Ye are not your own. For ye are bought with a price" (1 Corinthians 6:19, 20).

2. The Scriptures also teach that each believer is a steward and will some day give an account of his stewardship. Paul inferred this when he encouraged Timothy to charge the talented Ephesians that they "do good, that they be rich in good works, ready to distribute, willing to communicate; laying up in store for themselves a good foundation against the time to come" (1 Timothy 6:18, 19).

3. God, the Owner of all, amply provides for His stewards. His stewards, having food and raiment, are to be therewith content and are to use all else that he has for extending the kingdom of God (2 Corinthians 9:7-10).

4. God requires that the steward constantly recognize His ownership of the whole by the setting apart of a certain portion as an offering in worship (Deuteronomy 16:16, 17; 1 Corinthians 16:1, 2). The believer appearing empty before God in worship does not recognize the bountifulness of God (James 1:17). Those who do not regularly recognize their stewardship with a significant portion in worship are subject to covetousness which is very dangerous.

5. The faithful steward will bring an offering which is not marked by show or display (Matthew 6:3, 4). However, it will be liberal (Luke 6:38; 2 Corinthians 9:7), sacrificial (2 Samuel 24:24), systematic and proportionate (1 Corinthians 16:2; Deuteronomy 16:17).

The Christian idea of property is that the possession of property, whether little or great, is a sacred trust. This is in keeping with the total concept of Christian stewardship. This stands in conflict with two prominent worldly ideas: (1) the concept of "rugged individualism" which holds that every man should get what he can and use it as he pleases as long as he keeps the laws of society; and (2) socialism and communism which teach that the State should own and control all property for the common good and manage production and distribution even in defiance of moral restraints. These latter views encourage covetousness, but the Christian view brings all under submission to God. He is the owner of all we possess and only He should direct the use of it.

Jesus tells us a story of stewardship in Matthew 25:14-30. He tells of three men who were given a trust. Two of these men took in trust what their master offered and assumed the obligation which they owed to him. Although the master owed them nothing, he rewarded them liberally for their good stewardship. The third man was not so conscious of his obligation. He made no effort to improve upon what had been given to him in trust. As a result he was embarrassed before his master, and the master had him punished for his lack of effort. Even the talent which he had was taken from him. So we should learn the obligations which God has thrust upon us and assume all our responsibilities to use what He has entrusted to us.

II. THE OLD TESTAMENT TEACHES TITHING
(Genesis 14:17-24; 28:12-22; Deuteronomy 14:27-29; Malachi 3:7-15)

All of life is a stewardship. Time, talent, and opportunity are all main elements in this life. But one of the terms in which life may be expressed is money. Money is a measure of value as well as a medium of exchange. Although stewardship includes every possibility of life, all of its output both potential and actual, money in a certain sense can be used as a measure of a man's stewardship. The powers of body, mind, and soul are expended by a man to gain money. Money comes to a man's possession because he uses the output of his potential to gain it. When a man works for five dollars per hour he is selling his time, energy, and potential for that amount. So money does represent the stored-up power of a man.

Money should never be an end in life but only a means to gain worthy ends in life. Since man belongs to God, the gain of money through the expenditure of life, energy, and potential brings a responsibility to man. Tithing is the age old principle of giving account of one's gain to God. Tithing is not to be recognized as just a legal device for the support of a religious system. Tithing is an act of worship by the believer by which he recognizes God's ownership and claim to his life.

The Old Testament teaches tithing very explicitly. The first mention of tithing is found in Abraham's meeting with Melchizedek (Genesis 14:17-24). Abraham was a nomad and apparently had established no permanent place of worship. As head of his tribe he probably acted in the place of a priest when offerings were made for his family. This would appear to be the case at Bethel when he entered the land (Genesis 12:7, 8; 13:4) and at Hebron (13:18). When he met Melchizedek who undoubtedly was of like faith in the true God as Abraham, he seems to have felt obligated to pay tithe to this man. Melchizedek is presented as "the priest of the most high God" (14:18). Apparently this priest-king of Salem maintained a sanctuary in which worship to the true God was given. Here was a remnant of worshipers who worshiped as Abraham did. He wanted to worship God and give a token of his stewardship of life, so he did so by paying a tithe to him.

Although there is no evidence of just when the tithe was begun, it seems that it was a well-accepted custom at this time. This was a spontaneous act on the part of Abraham and not one in which he needed instruction. Here is a practice which antedates the law by several hundred years. Tithing, because of its antiquity in the Bible and also by its appearance in other religions, is recognized as the oldest system of religious giving on record.

In Genesis 28:20-22 is recorded the first pledge to tithe as a distinct part of a religious covenant with God. Jacob was fleeing the wrath of his brother Esau. He had bought the family birthright and stolen the father's blessing which belonged to his brother. Fearing for his life, he was going to his mother's people at Haran but stopped at Bethel to spend the night. It was here that he had the dream of the ladder reaching from earth to Heaven with angels ascending and descending. So impressed was he by this great dream, he made a vow to God. In the making of this vow, let us remember certain things. This experience of Jacob was not isolated from all prior events in his life. He had been with both Abraham and Isaac (Genesis 26:25) in worship. His actions here were a reflection of what he had learned from them. One of the key items in this experience is Jacob's pledge: "Of all that thou shalt give me I will surely give the tenth unto thee" (28:22). The fulfilment of his promise is found in Genesis 35:7 where it states that "he built there an altar." It may be that Jacob set up some permanent type of worship place here and used his tithe to sustain it. Bethel held a revered place among the Hebrews even in the days of Samuel (1 Samuel 7:16; 10:3).

Tithing was insisted upon in the Law of Moses. The Israelites were to give of the firstfruits of their children (Exodus 22:29, 30) and of their land (23:19). But above this they were to bring one-tenth of their increase to the temple. The command read, "There shall be a place which the LORD your God shall choose to cause his name to dwell there; thither shall ye bring all that I command you; your burnt offerings, and your sacrifices, your tithes, and the heave offering of your hand, and all your choice vows which ye vow unto the LORD" (Deuteronomy 12:11). It further read, "Thou shalt truly tithe all the increase of thy seed, that the field bringeth forth year by year" (Deuteronomy 14:22). It appears that a second tithe was given every third year for the law also read, "At the end of the three years thou shalt bring forth all the tithe of thine increase the same year" (14:28). This latter tithe appears to have been basically for benevolent purposes. Although the Levites were partakers of a share of it, it was not their main support.

The Levites were supported by the regular tithe. The Lord told Aaron, "I have given the children of Levi all the tenth in Israel for an inheritance, for their service which they serve, even the service of the tabernacle of the congregation" (Numbers 18:21). So the tithe given in worship by the children of Israel was the means by which the religion of the One True God was supported. This was true of both the tabernacle and the temple. The ministries of both required the services of a great number of priests and helpers, porters, singers, and keepers of the sacred vessels. These could not carry on their secular work while they served in the temple so the regular tithe was devoted to their support.

The prophet Amos mentions the tithe (4:4) and Nehemiah urged the people to tithe (10:38; 13:12). The last of the prophets, Malachi, is heard crying out against Israel for failing to tithe. To Israel he said, "Will a man rob God? Yet ye have robbed me. But ye say, Wherein have we robbed thee? In tithes and offerings. Ye are cursed with a curse: for ye have robbed me, even this whole nation" (3:8, 9). So the prophet saw failure to tithe as a great sin. It was the same as robbing God. The withholding of the tithe was a withholding from God of that which was His. It was not the money which God needed, although His ministries are not carried on as they should be when God's people fail to tithe. The big thing was that God's people were failing to worship Him as they should. In failing to worship by bringing the tithe, they were failing to recognize His ownership of them and all that they had.

The result to themselves of their failure to tithe was that they were "cursed with a curse" (verse 9). But Malachi gave the remedy to the situation in the same message. He added, "Bring ye all the tithes into the storehouse, that there may be meat in mine house, and prove me now herewith, saith the LORD of hosts, if I will not open you the windows of heaven, and pour you out a blessing, that there shall not be room enough to receive it" (Malachi 3:10). Tithing must be important if the doing of it brings a blessing this large. The prophet went on to define a part of this blessing, "I will rebuke the devourer for your sakes, and he shall not destroy the fruits of your ground; neither shall your vine cast her fruit before the time in the field, saith the LORD of hosts. And all nations shall call you blessed: for ye shall be a delightsome land" (3:11, 12).

So tithing in the Old Testament was a key to the religious life of the people. When they did not tithe they were showing (1) a disinterest in the work of the Lord and (2) were failing to acknowledge His priority in their lives. Two awful things resulted: (1) Their spiritual lives depreciated and spiritual things became of lesser importance. (2) The worship and the service of the Lord was neglected and fell into disgrace. The total result was a collapse of the moral structure of the nation.

Blessings always grow out of a proper relationship with God. This gives confidence to a man as well as purpose in life. The blessing too large to receive, however, is that plus element when God's presence is with man. Israel always found prosperity and security when they walked in God's ways. Trouble and ultimately destruction came to their nation when they forgot God and went after their own ways. Failing to tithe was just an evidence of their refusing God.

III. THE NEW TESTAMENT TEACHES TITHING
(2 Corinthians 9:1-12; 1 Corinthians 16:1, 2)

The motive for a person's gift is very important. Love of Christ and thanksgiving for the grace of Christ is a worthy motive which has already been given. A false motive is one that teaches that if we give God a dollar, He will give us more back in return. It is true that God has promised His blessings on the tither (Malachi 3:10-12). But those blessings do not come on a dollar per dollar return in accordance to how we have given. Our motivation should not be that we give just because it is a commandment or requirement. As long as any person gives for these reasons, the real blessedness in giving is lost.

Our possessions are not our own. Therefore, we do not have the right to determine their use. The Owner of them is another and therefore the decision is made for us. The purpose for the tithe is that human and spiritual needs might be met through the church. Because we are born again Christians, we should want to see these needs met through the church. We should realize that the tithe is our means of contributing to the fulfilment of those needs. If believers in a church adopt tithing and give according to the following principles, just think of the potential the church would have! Note these principles:

1. Give self before giving money. This is a principle which Paul set before the Macedonian churches. Writing to them he held up the Philippian believers as an example and said that they first "gave their own selves to the Lord" (2 Corinthians 8:5). When all of self is given, the rest will take care of itself. However, the gift without the giver is bare. Giving to God must first be a giving of self.

2. Give according to ability. Jesus commended the widow for giving her two mites. This was because the gift represented more than she could have given normally and without sacrifice. Paul said that a gift is "accepted according to that a man hath, not according to that he hath not" (2 Corinthians 8:12). Our gifts are acceptable when given according to ability whether large or small.

3. Give according to a regular pattern. Energetic giving this year will not suffice for next year's neglect. The responsibilities of your church are constant. Paul recommended giving "upon the first day of the week" (1 Corinthians 16:2). This can be a "firstfruit" giving. We should always take the tithe before we try to meet our other bills.

4. Give with a joyful heart. Paul tells us that "God loveth a cheerful giver" (2 Corinthians 9:7). Paul wrote of the giving of the Macedonians which though it came out of "a great trial of affliction the abundance of their joy and their deep poverty abounded

unto the riches of their liberality" (2 Corinthians 8:2). God does not want us to give "grudgingly, or of necessity" (2 Corinthians 9:7). When such pressure is put upon a person, joy is killed. Paul's principle was to give "every man according as he purposeth in his heart." This, of course, was with the tithe serving as a basic amount.

5. Every believer should give generously. Paul said, "He which soweth sparingly shall reap also sparingly; and he which soweth bountifully shall reap also bountifully" (2 Corinthians 9:6). Stingy sowing will bring no generous rewards. The principle, "whatsoever a man soweth that shall he also reap" can be applied here. If you sow a little, you reap a little. We reap what we sow, and our reaping will be in accord with our generosity in sowing.

6. Give with sacrifice. Christianity has tended in our modern days to leave sacrifice out of service. Sacrifice should be a part of believers' giving, however. Just as the believers in Macedonia gave "beyond their power," so should we. Our giving should not be "as of covetousness" (2 Corinthians 9:5). It is wonderful to note that tithers are rarely selfish, greedy, narrow, proud, covetous, or self-centered. It is the tither who always feels rather that he is not giving enough but should give more and more.

When a church gives according to God's plan, the following things can be expected:

1. The church will have "all sufficiency in all things" (2 Corinthians 9:8). This will enable the church to "abound to every good work." They won't have to devote themselves to fund raising but can turn to spiritual pursuits.

2. The church will be "enriched in every thing in all bountifulness." They will be enriched spiritually because giving is a spiritual exercise. The bountiful spirit which results will affect every area of church life.

3. "The want of the saints" will be supplied (verse 12). Church benevolent work will be accomplished because the means are at

hand. Most churches have had to leave benevolent work up to the government for lack of funds. This should not be true.

4. God is glorified by the subjection of the church to His will in the matter of giving. Increased witness, greater benevolent giving, and related activities will just naturally bring greater glory to God.

5. Paying tithes is a means of witness that Jesus is alive (Hebrews 7:8). Tithes are paid to men who are alive and worthy to receive the tithe.

Tithing is a sensible and reasonable means of supporting the church. Believers should study the doctrine and accept the challenge of giving through this means.

Although Paul does not specifically mention the tithe in 1 Corinthians 16:1, 2, it seems evident that he was speaking of the tithe. Like the tithe the gifts given were to be systematic, "upon the first day of the week." All believers should have a set time that they give of their income to the Lord's service. On the day of worship is the ideal time each week to set aside that part which testifies to God's ownership of our lives.

The offering Paul described was to be proportionate for every person: "as God hath prospered him." Tithing is proportionate giving. When each person gives ten percent of that with which God has prospered him, the gift of that person is as large as the gift of any other. Proportionate giving is a fair means of giving which God has ordained.

When giving is systematic and proportionate and according to God's plan, it relieves the church of many problems. When people do not tithe, the church officials often turn to fund raising which does not bring glory to God. Pie bakes and chili suppers are wonderful for fellowship and some purposes, but they detract from God's honor when they are used to displace God's financial plan of support of His work. Paul wanted no "gatherings when I come." When frantic means are used to raise finances for the extension of the kingdom of God, it makes God look poor. It makes His people appear as if they were not living out of the bountiful hand of God. There is every reason to believe that the same blessings promised Israel through Malachi will also come upon the church that follows God's plan.

A final argument from the New Testament for tithing is found in contrast to Old Testament giving. If God required ten percent under the law, can anyone suppose that the love that went to the cross demands from believers a smaller gift than the people who brought their tithes to the ancient altars of Israel? The New Testament teaches that salvation is free; but when a person is saved, his heart should so overflow with joy and thankfulness that he wants to see the kingdom of God spread. So the grace of the New Testament should be the compelling teaching which leads every believer, not just to want to give a tenth as required by the law, but to give as much as he can.

IV. TITHING IS GOD'S FINANCIAL PLAN FOR THE SUPPORT OF HIS WORK (1 Corinthians 9:1-18)

In the New Testament a different situation exists to that in the Old Testament. In the Old Testament the law gives the specific command, "Thou shalt truly tithe" (Deuteronomy 14:22). Many who study the Bible refuse to teach tithing because it is not so specifically commanded in the New Testament. But if we will only notice, the commands of the law are not stated as direct commands in the New Testament. Nowhere do we have a Decalogue of Commands as is given in the Old Testament nor a Levitical system of commands as is found there. But notice the following arguments for the tithe in the New Testament.

The tithe is in no place in the New Testament challenged, disproved, or set aside. Jesus Himself said, "Think not that I am come to destroy the law, or the prophets: I am not come to destroy, but to fulfil" (Matthew 5:17). Of course, the ceremonial law was fulfilled in His death and was no longer necessary; therefore it passed away. But the tithing principle was different. Being in effect from before the law, it was a principle that in time will always be in effect. It was made a part of the law for this reason.

Jesus put His stamp of approval on tithing. Although He condemned the scribes and Pharisees for giving extremely minute attention to tithing while omitting "weightier matters of the law" (Matthew 23:23), He did go on to support tithing. His statement was: "These ought ye to have done [the tithing of the herbs that grew in the garden], and not to leave the other undone." There is no other way to interpret this than that He was giving His full support to tithing as a means of supporting the service and worship of God.

The principles that undergird tithing as a means of supporting the work of the Lord are evident throughout the New Testament. The same concept of divine ownership and human stewardship are proclaimed constantly. In the parable of the talents (Matthew 25:15-30) stewardship is taught. This is true also in the parable of the pounds (Luke 19:13-15). Did not Paul teach divine ownership when he wrote: "Ye are not your own. For ye are bought with a price" (1 Corinthians 6:19-20)?

In 1 Corinthians 9:7-18 Paul gives several arguments for the support of the ministry. He gives an argument from natural analogy: "Who goeth a warfare any time at his own charges? who planteth a vineyard, and eateth not of the fruit thereof?" He gives also a scriptural argument: "Or saith not the law the same also? For it is written in the law of Moses, Thou shalt not muzzle the mouth of the ox that treadeth out the corn." He turned then to an argument from inherent justice by saying: "He that ploweth should plow in hope; and that he that thresheth in hope should he partaker of his hope."

Paul turned also to common practice for an argument. He said, "If we have sown unto you spiritual things, is it a great thing if we shall reap your carnal things? If others be partakers of this power over you, are not we rather?" Doctors, teachers, and government officials are paid for their services, why not the minister?

From these he then turned to two clinching arguments: (1) It was the Old Testament custom to support those who ministered about spiritual things. In verse 13 he said, "Do ye not know that they which minister about holy things live of the things of the temple? and they which wait at the altar are partakers with the altar?" (2) The Lord Jesus Christ commanded that the ministry be supported. In verse 14 Paul said, "Even so hath the Lord ordained that they which preach the gospel should live of the gospel."

In keeping with these arguments for the faithful support of the ministry, let us note the following things: (1) The New Testament nowhere does away with tithing as a means of support of the worship and service of God. (2) The New Testament at no place provides for an alternate plan of support for the Church. (3) The New Testament seems to assume that tithing is the accepted means of support of the gospel ministry.

Paul did not expect this privilege for himself and did not use it (verse 15). We may be sure that every preacher is like Paul and feels compelled to preach the gospel regardless of whether he is supported or not (verse 16), but still it is a New Testament principle.

10

The Call and Responsibility of the Ministry

BACKGROUND

Christianity was ushered into the world by a preacher. John the Baptist came preaching, "Prepare ye the way of the Lord." His was a divine mission, and he readily acknowledged his calling.

Such preaching, however, was not new. The Jewish people had been visited by other great preachers, Elijah, Isaiah, and Jeremiah to name a few.

It was God's way, when He wished to convey His message to men, to use men as His spokesmen. Even before Christianity, God called men to proclaim His message.

When Jesus began His ministry, He began it preaching that men must repent. As He gathered others to Himself, He instructed them and sent them forth to preach.

The record in Acts is a record of the Holy Spirit's empowering all Christians to witness and calling men into the special work of preaching the gospel.

In the light of these enumerated facts, how can anyone scoff at the idea that God still calls men into the ministry? There are some, however, who deny that there is such a thing as a divine call.

Free Will Baptists believe in a divine call to the ministry. If an individual has any doubts about his calling, he has no business trying to be an ordained minister.

In spite of this belief in a divine call, there is a dearth of ministers in the Free Will Baptist denomination. There needs to be more stress laid on the subject of God's call to special service. If God is still calling, and He is, someone is refusing to obey. How much better it is to say with Paul, "I was not disobedient unto the heavenly vision.

Volumes have been written, and many more could be written, about the history of Christian preaching. There have been many great men of God since the days of the apostles who used the Sword of the Spirit with power and demonstration of the Holy Spirit.

There are still good and great men today who are doing the same thing. They may be in the minority, but they are still to be found and will be found until the end of time.

The prayer of all Christians should be for God to raise up more men who will proclaim the truth without fear or favor, without compromise or concession. God give us such men!

OUTLINE

I. The Call of the Minister (Matthew 4:18-22)
II. The Qualifications of the Minister (1 Timothy 3:1-7; Titus 1)
III. The Duties of the Minister (2 Timothy 4:1-5)

INTRODUCTION

Does God speak to the hearts of individuals and call them to specific ministries? This question is asked because there are many in Christendom today who deny this fact. Before answering the question, one needs to recognize one important thing. Every believer has the privilege and responsibility to spread the gospel message wherever he goes. The propagation of the saving message of Christ was never intended to be left to the few but was to be the duty of all believers throughout their lives. Men, women, and children are obligated to bear witness through the enabling grace of the Holy Spirit of what Christ has done for their lives.

The service of these need not take the form of preaching or going to the mission field or some other specific ministry. Their witness is to be casual as they carry on their every day pursuits in life.

But how about a specific call to the ministry of preaching? Is there such a thing? Liberals would tell us that the ministry is to be chosen as any other occupation. They base this on the idea that God does not speak to people to give specific calls to the ministry. This lesson is designed to present Free Will Baptists' views regarding the call to the ministry, the qualifications in a man that will enable us to recognize that he has been called, and the responsibilities of the person who has been called. Let us look to the Scriptures for the answers to the question.

I. THE CALL OF THE MINISTER
(Matthew 4:18-22)

The Old Testament is filled with the story of men who claimed to hold a special commission from the Lord to speak for Him. Isaiah tells us that a seraph touched his lips with a live coal off the temple altar and that the voice of the Lord said, "Whom shall I send, and who will go for us? Then said I, Here am I; send me" (Isaiah 6:8). After his response to God, he was commanded to go and preach to the people.

In the first chapter of his book, Jeremiah tells about a special experience with the Lord. In that experience Jeremiah gives us the

145

details of his call. He reported, "Then the word of the LORD came unto me, saying, Before I formed thee in the belly I knew thee; and before thou camest forth out of the womb I sanctified thee, and I ordained thee a prophet unto the nations. Then said I, Ah, Lord GOD! behold, I cannot speak; for I am a child. But the LORD said unto me, Say not, I am a child: for thou shalt go to all that I shall send thee, and whatsoever I command thee thou shalt speak. Be not afraid of their faces: for I am with thee to deliver thee, saith the LORD. Then the LORD put forth his hand, and touched my mouth. And the LORD said unto me, Behold, I have put my words in thy mouth. See, I have this day set thee over the nations and over the kingdoms, to root out, and to pull down, and to destroy, and to throw down, and to build, and to plant" (1:4-10).

The call of Ezekiel is very similar to that of Jeremiah and Isaiah. To him the Lord said, "Son of man, I send thee to the children of Israel, to a rebellious nation that hath rebelled against me" (Ezekiel 2:3). Later the Lord said unto him, "Son of man, go, get thee unto the house of Israel, and speak with my words unto them" (3:4).

It was Paul who so well described the call to the ministry in the New Testament. In Romans 10:14, 15 he wrote, "How then shall they call on him in whom they have not believed? and how shall they believe in him of whom they have not heard? and how shall they hear without a preacher? And how shall they preach, except they be sent?"

The call which Jesus issued to certain men to become His disciples is typical of God's call to men. Four of the first men Jesus called were Peter, Andrew, James, and John. These men had probably all met Jesus and gotten acquainted with Him in Judea through the ministry of John the Baptist (John 1:35). But it was later when Jesus was preaching in the area of the Sea of Galilee that Jesus called these men to become His disciples.

Jesus called these four fishermen in a unique fashion. "Follow me, and I will make you fishers of men" was the gist of His address to them. Matthew's account omits the prior knowledge which they had of Him, but they had already met Him and received Him as the Messiah. How well they knew Him can only be supposed; however, they knew Him well enough to accept Him as the promised Messiah for "they straightway left their nets, and followed him" (Matthew 4:20). Practically the same thing is said of James and John. Of their call it is stated that "he called them" (verse 21). Of their response it is reported, "They immediately left the ship and their father, and followed him" (verse 22).

There is much more to these calls than is generally viewed from a casual reading. These men were called to be disciples or learners. To follow Jesus was to accept Him for what He claimed to be and after learning from Him to go forth representing Him. To accept the invitation of Jesus to "follow me" involved a great decision for these men. They were laboring men. His call was to leave their fisherman's occupation and to employ themselves in His service. They were to become full time "fishers of men." They had to forsake their occupation to become His disciples. Later one of them said, "Lo, we have left all, and have followed thee."

These disciples (learners) were to become apostles (sent forth ones). They were not only to accept the message of Christ and learn about it, they were to become supporters of it who went forth assisting in the spread of His message and teachings. So to answer the call was quite involved. This was true also in the call of others such as Philip (John 1:43) and Matthew (Matthew 9:9).

Other names given to the minister in the New Testament imply a previous call to that office. Paul wrote on one occasion, "We are ambassadors for Christ" (2 Corinthians 5:20). The very essence of the ambassadorial position is found in the fact that he is given an appointment by the person he represents. So the minister as an ambassador is called and commissioned for his office. This is supported by Paul's statement that God "hath committed to us the word of reconciliation" (verse 19).

In an earlier book Paul had used other terms for the same office. He said, "Let a man so account of us, as of the ministers of Christ, and stewards of the mysteries of God" (1 Corinthians 4:1). A minister is an attendant or servant. A steward holds an office from one who is his master. One does not choose to be a steward but is made one when the master elects to entrust either goods or a responsibility to him. So the one called to the ministry is a "steward of God" (Titus 1:7).

Timothy was urged to "make full proof of thy ministry" (2 Timothy 4:5). If he had no calling or stewardship to prove, the meaning of this statement is useless.

The "gifts" of God listed in Ephesians 4:11 represent certain men set apart for particular callings. Some men then were called and endowed to be apostles, prophets, evangelists, pastors, and teachers. Of Paul it was said by God, "He is a chosen vessel unto me, to bear my name before the Gentiles" (Acts 9:15).

Since Jesus is not on earth to walk by the place of a person's employment and call him from that vocation to His ministry, the question might be asked, "Just how does God call men to the ministry?" Charles Spurgeon listed three things which were evidence of a call: (1) An intense, all-absorbing desire for the work. This he described as an "overwhelming craving and raging thirst for telling to others what God has done to our souls." (2) An aptness to teach and other qualities which would enable one to carry on the work of the ministry. (3) A measure of response in His efforts to witness for Christ.

Probably more men are called through a growing experience than in any other way. There grows an abiding conviction of which one cannot rid his life that he must give himself to Christ's ministry. However, there are some men who receive the call through a sudden or outstanding spiritual experience. Paul's call was of this nature. However, one should avoid seeking an experience just like another minister's. All are not called alike. One who has a series of impressionable experiences is just as called as the man of whom I heard that "wrestled down two acres of corn." Of one thing we may be sure, the person will be aware of his call. The problem arises when some men miss their calling. Every man should be positive that he is called to the gospel ministry before he assumes it.

II. THE QUALIFICATIONS OF THE MINISTER
(1 Timothy 3:1-7; Titus 1)

For the qualifications of a minister the *Free Will Baptist Treatise* has the following to say: "They must possess good, natural and acquired abilities, deep and ardent piety, be especially called of God to the work, and ordained by prayer and the laying on of hands." This is a general statement and covers many things. Note the four things listed:

1. *Natural and acquired abilities.* The natural abilities are those with which a man is endowed at birth. It would be good for every man entering the ministry to have a capacity for clear thinking with strong feelings. He should have a vigorous imagination which by using he can apply the gospel to every life he enters. The minister needs to be endowed with a capacity for expressing his message with power.

Since all men are not equally endowed with these natural abilities, some must try harder to acquire certain abilities to make up for their lack. Skills, such as the choice, collection, and arrangement of materials as well as good delivery, are ones which can be acquired by hard work. Also a minister should develop his knowledge of religious truth and human nature. This is why Paul urged the minister to "Study to shew thyself approved unto God, a workman that needeth not to be ashamed, rightly dividing the word of truth" (2 Timothy 2:15).

2. A *deep and ardent piety*. The minister should be a deeply religious person. Piety is quality of soul. It is devoutness to the Savior he serves. It is faithfulness of one's obligations in Christ. No man can be successful in the ministry whose service for Christ is not the foremost thing in his life.

3. A *call from God*. No man should enter the ministry as an occupation or profession. It is not purely a vocation. It is a life devoted to a special calling. When a man stands to preach, he should stand there with the knowledge that he represents the Lord Jesus Christ and has a message from Him. This call is more than a call for every believer to witness. It is the distinct impression made on a person that he must devote his life to preaching the gospel of Christ.

4. *Ordination by laying on of hands*. Ordination by man does not impart any special grace or power to one called of God. Ordination is the recognition of God's people that there are evidences of a divine call in a man's life. It is the ceremony in the church by which public recognition of this call is given. Those who teach apostolic succession believe that the laying on of hands is necessary for one in a succession from the apostles (Peter for the Catholics). But the laying on of hands can be done by anyone designated by the church and represents the authority to preach granted by the church.

It is to the Scriptures themselves that we must turn for the specific qualifications of the minister. These are preserved for us in Paul's writings to Timothy and Titus. These have been used by the churches as guidelines through the centuries. Paul begins his discussion of those qualifications by saying: "If a man desire the office of a bishop, he desireth a good work" (1 Timothy 3:1). The desire that he mentions is that godly desire of which Paul had spoken when he wrote to the Corinthians saying, "Covet earnestly the best gifts" (1 Corinthians 12:31). He did not say that one received the call to the ministry because he desired it. One does not make the choice. God does. However, men in the church who are capable of the office should desire it earnestly and even pray for it.

The "office of a bishop" is referred to by many other terms in the Bible. One of these terms is *elder*. This was a title of respect paid to older men in Jewry and was brought over into the Christian movement. It came to apply to persons in high official position and suggests the dignity and gravity of the office.

The word *pastor* is also used. It comes from the word meaning shepherd and is a tender and affectionate title. It is mentioned in Ephesians 4:11. The word *minister* is another biblical term used today for the bishop. It is a word which originally referred to a very lowly servant. It often referred to one who went on an errand bearing a message. It is a very appropriate title for the preacher. Other terms used of the bishop are servant translated minister, (1 Corinthians 3:5; 2 Corinthians 3:6; Ephesians 3:7), steward (1 Corinthians 4:1; 1 Timothy 3:15), brother (Acts 9:17), and evangelist (Ephesians 4:11). Also included in these titles could be apostle (Ephesians 1:1; Colossians 1:1), prophet (1 Corinthians 12:28), teacher (1 Corinthians 12:28; Ephesians 4:11), and preacher (Romans 10:14; 1 Timothy 2:7). The qualifications for the person described are listed as follows in 1 Timothy 3:2-7:

Blameless. This word comes from an adjective which means "not to be taken hold of" and implies faultlessness. This does not mean that a person is not a criminal but that no one can place a finger on anything that would injure his reputation. It suggests a consistent, mature Christian life with no occasion in it for rebuke or reproach.

Husband of one wife. There are five chief interpretations of this passage: (1) One is that it simply prohibits polygamy and a bishop cannot be husband of more than one wife at a time. (2) A common view in some parts of the world is that Paul was prohibiting bishops from remarrying after their first wife died. (3) One view is that the minister must have one wife and a single man could not fill the office. Only married men are eligible for ordination under this view. (4) Another interpretation would prohibit any person from taking this office if he was divorced or had any other record of marital infidelity. (5) The Roman Catholics' view is that marriage was prohibited and the "one wife" to which the bishop was married was the Church.

Although Free Will Baptists have different opinions, the majority would seem to follow the fourth view which prohibits divorcees from holding the office. Although this is true, many associations make allowances for what is referred to as "biblical grounds for divorce." Since the Scriptures hold extremely high standards for the office, the passage seems to prohibit anyone from assuming the office who has any past record of divorce or marital infidelity, even before conversion. A background problem in this area would violate the qualification of blamelessness.

Vigiliant. This word is one that is used of abstaining from wine entirely but seems here to mean more since that qualification is dealt with later. It probably means "spiritually sober, temperate, calm, and sober in judgment." It refers to a life which follows active sobriety and watchfulness.

Sober. This word in the Greek refers to a person who is self-restrained or discreet. This is a quality of mind found in one who is serious and earnest. We often use it to refer to a man who is sound in judgments.

Of good behaviour. The center reference of the King James Version uses the term "modest" but this does not bring out the main force of the word. It refers rather to a life which is well-ordered. It means an orderliness in the physical, moral, and mental life of a person.

Given to hospitality. The root of this word actually means "a lover of strangers." In the early days this attribute was one of importance. With no motels and hotels to speak of, the entertainment of traveling brethren was a necessity. Persecution, poverty, and flight from the brawls and vice of the inns of that day gave a great opportunity for service in this work.

Apt to teach. Aptitude here refers to an ability to teach or to impart knowledge to others. Teaching is a vital part of any ministry, especially preaching. This suggests two qualities: ability to teach and knowledge of something to teach. Training and education developes skill in teaching.

Not given to wine. This word can be used without reference to wine. It probably refers to a character rather than the mere fact of abstaining from wine. It can be translated "not a brawler" or not one who drinks and becomes quarrelsome after drinking.

No striker. The bishop should not be an evil-tempered individual who quickly strikes back with his fists when annoyed. This term sets forth the opposite of what a Christian is as the word *patient* in this verse shows. The Christian will have more annoyances than the unbeliever, so he especially must be careful of his quick temper.

Not greedy of filthy lucre. The minister has a right to the support of his people (1 Corinthians 9:7.15), but he should not be desirous of unfair gain. The usefulness of a minister is paralyzed when money becomes the driving force in his life. As an example of all believers, he needs to be free from domination by material possessions and goods.

Patient. This word stands especially in contrast to "no striker" and "not a brawler" which follows. The minister is forbearing. He should be reasonable and gentle in all situations, even when provoked by worldly men. Such a disposition will avoid conflict with the world.

Not a brawler. Like "striker" this denotes a contentious person, one who is always aggressive and on the offensive. While insisting on his rights, he is not always able to keep his temper under control. Paul seems to be describing the right character trait when he said, "The servant of the Lord must not strive; but be gentle unto all men" (2 Timothy 2:24).

Not covetous. Because this attribute is very similar to "not given to filthy lucre," this latter is often omitted from texts of the Bible. Covetousness is probably a broader term than the other, however. It stands in contrast to the liberality which should mark a minister of Christ. A covetous person or lover of money is apt to give himself to filthy lucre rather than to Christ's service.

Rules well his house. The manner in which a man governs his home will reveal his capacity for leadership in the church. Superintending the house of God is an even greater task than making a home run smoothly, but one successful in the home has at least marked himself as capable of demanding respect.

Not a novice. The word means "newly planted." It probably refers here to a new convert, a person who has not reached maturity in spiritual things. An immature person is likely to be inflated with pride and fall if given too much responsibility. "Lay hands suddenly on no man" is still a good admonition. Conceit is especially a trait of the immature and inexperienced.

Of good report among outsiders. Reputation and character are two different things. Paul has been dealing with character—what a man really is. He now mentions reputation—what people think you are. If a minister is going to have success, he must have a good reputation. Reproach or accusation is difficult to take, unless one is above reproach. Satan snares those who are unwary and who permit things which smear their names. When there is a buildup of unfavorable opinion about a man, the pressures become very heavy and may cause a man to fall.

The list of qualifications which Paul sent to Titus are similar to these (Titus 1:7-9). Titus in Crete was to use the same standards as Timothy in Ephesus. Note the similarities and only slight differences in the passages.

III. THE DUTIES OF THE MINISTER
(2 Timothy 4:1-5)

"Preach the word" is the first and basic duty of any man called to the ministry. All other duties fall to second place as one heralds the message given to him by his Lord. Kent in his comment on this verse said, "He must announce it in its completeness (Acts 20:27), without alteration, addition, or subtraction. He must proclaim, not philosophize or argue. This message is the Word of God, which has previously been explained as God-breathed Scripture (2 Timothy 3:16, 17). To proclaim God's Word involves all the themes of Scripture, not picking out some and ignoring others. The Word of God in its entirety is the basic material of the preacher's message."

The seriousness of this admonition to preach the Word is found in the preceding verse. The charge by Paul to Timothy was given "before God, and the Lord Jesus Christ." It was not just encouragement from one man to another. It was the solemn charge from an experienced spiritual leader who was trying to impress on a younger man the seriousness of his call to the ministry. He had a calling and a responsibility to that calling. His duty was to "preach the Word," to herald the message of the one who called him.

Adding to the gravity of this duty was the fact of who it was who called him. Jesus Christ was the one who would "judge the quick and the dead at his appearing and his kingdom." These to whom Timothy was to preach were soon to face judgment and needed to make peace with the one who would judge them.

Timothy was urged to "be instant in season, out of season." The concept in "be instant" is to stand by or to be ready. Whether it is appropriate or seemingly inappropriate, opportune or inopportune, the minister's duty is to preach the Word. A minister is never off duty. He should always be ready to press the claims of Christ on a lost world.

Three things the minister is supposed to do, using the Word of God: (1) *Reprove.* By applying the Word of God to the lives of sinners, their violation of God's standard and will are pointed out to bring conviction of sin to them. The purpose of reproof should always be to bring men to a conviction of their guilt before God and to convince them of their need for Christ as Savior. Reproof which only stirs to anger is no good. It must bring conviction of a need.

(2) *Rebuke.* This word goes further than the previous one. It involves actual censure and a placing of blame. It is a word used in the New Testament of expressing a judgment on what is contrary or wrong. It is the presentation of arguments to one to convince him of what is truth. The propriety of such rebuke lies in one's authority to rebuke. The believer has no authority in himself or in his own opinion. It is only as he uses the Word that he has an authority to place blame upon another. The Word of God condemns sin and is a rebuke when presented.

(3) *Exhort.* Exhortation is the presenting of encouragement and comfort. This word comes from the same root from which the word *Comforter* as applied to the Holy Spirit is derived. As the Holy Spirit is a Comforter or one called alongside to help, so the minister is to take those who respond to rebuke and give them encouragement in the right way. This can be done by using the Word to show how sins are forgiven and how one's spiritual life can be strengthened.

The duties of a minister are continued in verse 5. Paul adds there, "Watch thou in all things." Just as the minister was to be characterized by vigilance and sobriety (Titus 1:8; 2:11-13), so his duty is to be watchful and alert. Vigilance should be pointed in two directions. The man of God should be alert to every opportunity to declare the Word. This Paul had referred to in verse 2. Here it is probably pointing back to verses 3 and 4. The minister must always be alert to the attacks of those who have wrong motives and false teachings. These are the ones who will turn others to fables and falsehoods.

The duty of a minister will also demand that he "endure afflictions." The bearing of burdens will sometimes be private, his own (Galatians 6:5). At times he must bear the burdens of others (Galatians 6:2). Sometimes the suffering will go beyond that of merely bearing a load of burdens. Paul invited Timothy to join him as a "partaker of the afflictions of the gospel" as he languished in a death cell in Rome. Peter urged, "But let none of you suffer as a murderer, or as a thief, or as an evildoer, or as a busybody in other men's matters. Yet if any man suffer as a Christian, let him not be ashamed; but let him glorify God on this behalf" (1 Peter 4:15, 16). He also said, "Let them that suffer according to the will of God commit the keeping of their souls to him in well doing, as unto a faithful Creator" (verse 19).

The minister, according to Paul, is to "do the work of an evangelist." The gift of evangelizing was a special endowment for proclaiming the good news of salvation. Although it may be a special calling to some (Philip, Acts 21:8; Ephesians 4:11), it is also the obligation of all who are called to preach. The pastor cannot forget the unsaved. It is the task of the missionary to be concerned with the redemption of men's souls. To whatsoever area of service a person is called, a vital part of his work will always be to announce the good news of redemption through the shed blood of Christ.

Then Paul said, "Make full proof of thy ministry." The margin reads, "Fulfill thy ministry." The suggestion seems to be to carry out fully your ministry. Make sure that all elements of the ministry are conscientiously performed whether it be teaching, pastoring, exhorting, or evangelizing. God does not want half-hearted service.

The *Free Will Baptist Treatise* says that the duties of ministers are to "preach the Word, administer the ordinances of the Gospel, visit their people, and otherwise perform the work of faithful ministers." We might say that the minister is "to be ready to every good work."

The work of the minister is complicated by the false ministers whom Paul says "shall turn away their ears from the truth, and shall be turned unto fables" (2 Timothy 4:4). Because men are not anxious to be molded by "sound doctrine," they tend to respond to these ministers more readily than to those who preach the truth. To Titus Paul wrote of these false teachers, "Rebuke them sharply, that they may be sound in the faith" (Titus 1:13). The minister may not always relish the fight and the opposition to these false prophets, but if he "makes full proof of his ministry," it will involve some defense of the faith. This is why Jude wrote that we should "earnestly contend for the faith." The minister must present the truth against those who "profess that they know God but in works they deny him" (Titus 1:16).

The duties of the man of God might be summed up in the words of Solomon who wrote, "Whatsoever thy hand findeth to do, do it with thy might" (Ecclesiastes 9:10).

11

The Ordinances of the Gospel

BACKGROUND

Because of the error which entered Christianity regarding baptism and its relationship to regeneration (it was believed by some that sins could not be removed without water baptism), the error regarding the mode took hold of the minds of many. The first record of any mode besides immersion is that of pouring. The man was too sick to be immersed and because the belief in baptismal regeneration was held by those involved, the pouring was substituted—not without protest by many others. One error leads to many.

Today these two errors on the mode and the purpose still exist. Free Will Baptists need to be firmly grounded in the Word of God and know what the Bible teaches concerning baptism.

Perhaps the verse which has troubled more people than any other is Acts 2:38. An examination of the Greek text reveals an interesting fact. The word *repent* is a plural word while the phrase "be baptized" is singular. The phrase "remission of sins" is also plural, referring to the sins of all who are being addressed. The verse could be translated literally, "All of you repent (and let each one be baptized) unto the remission of the sins of all of you. . . ." This

159

would place remission of the sins of all contingent upon the repentance of all and baptism a natural consequence for each one to observe as a result of his salvation.

The ordinance of washing the saints' feet has not been observed by most denominations. Some say that the early church did not observe this ordinance. Dummelow states in his commentary that this precept was literally obeyed by many ancient churches.

Benjamin Randall believed in and practiced the ordinance. It was in the next century that the northern group (who took the name Free Baptists to express their opposition to slavery) voted to leave the practice to the decision of each local church.

Our heritage is one that embraces the ordinance. Our *Treatise* states plainly that we believe it to be an ordinance. But, most important, the Bible clearly teaches it. Whether or not there are any customs and traditions, if the Bible teaches a particular doctrine, we should accept it and perpetuate it. "The servant is not greater than his lord."

Some would insist that Jesus was merely observing a custom of the time. They fail to point out that the custom was for the feet to be washed before entering the house. This act took place in an upper room. It was not a custom by any stretch of the imagination.

OUTLINE

I. Baptism (Romans 6:1-5)
II. The Lord's Supper (Matthew 26:26-29; 1 Corinthians 11:23-30)
III. Washing The Saints' Feet (John 13:2-17)

INTRODUCTION

As individual believers lose spiritual power through increased materialism and association with the world, the trend of the churches is toward a sacerdotal religion. This is a religion which depends upon the sacraments. A sacrament is something presented to the senses which has the power by divine institution of conveying grace. It is supposed that grace from God is conveyed by observing certain rites and ceremonies. The Catholic Church has seven such sacraments which purportedly convey grace.

Free Will Baptists do not believe in sacraments, but they do have three gospel ordinances which they teach. An ordinance is an outward rite appointed by Christ as a visible sign of the saving truth of the Christian faith. These three ordinances combine to set forth the central truths of the Christian faith. As prescribed in the New Testament they are baptism, the Lord's Supper, and feet washing.

Three facts determine what constitutes an ordinance: (1) It was ordained by Christ. (2) It sets forth a central truth of the gospel. (3) It was intended to be perpetuated continually in the church.

I. BAPTISM
(Romans 6:1-5)

The *Treatise* defines Christian baptism as "the immersion of believers in water, in the name of the Father, the Son, and the Holy Spirit, in which is represented the burial and resurrection of Christ, the death of Christians to the world, the washing of their souls from the pollution of sin, their rising to newness of life, their engagement to serve God, and their resurrection at the last day."

The approval of Jesus was stamped on baptism when He submitted to the baptism of John (Matthew 3:13-15). Although John was hesitant to baptize Jesus, He insisted upon going through the ordinance "to fulfil all righteousness." By submitting to baptism He set an example for all believers of all ages since.

Those who came to Jesus and became His followers were baptized (John 4:1, 2). It does not appear that Jesus baptized, but He gave the privilege to His disciples who baptized others who followed Him.

It is in the Great Commission that the specific command to baptize is given by Jesus. In it He said, "Go ye therefore, and teach all nations, baptizing them in the name of the Father, and of the Son, and of the Holy Ghost" (Matthew 28:19). Coupled as it is to the Great Commission, it must be of vital importance for it to be observed. It is always linked very closely with salvation for Jesus said, "He that believeth and is baptized shall be saved" (Mark 16:16).

The passage for study in today's lesson shows how vitally linked that baptism is to salvation. The ordinance is a symbol of the believer's identification with Christ in His burial and resurrection (Romans 6:1-5). It is important for us to realize that the believer's identification with Christ is not effected by the rite of baptism.

Baptism functions to symbolize that salvation event which brings the Christian into personal contact with Christ. It does this through a series of acts which correspond to the redeeming acts of Christ.

Immersion symbolizes Death.

Submersion symbolizes Burial.

Emergence symbolizes Resurrection.

In the actual experience of salvation the believer dies out to self and the old life. The old man or old nature is buried. By the new birth the believer is resurrected to a new life. It is these spiritual experiences that are symbolized by baptism.

Baptism is symbolic of the act which brings us "into Jesus Christ" (Romans 6:3). This describes the closest allegiance and adhesion to Him. In our baptism we profess obedience to Christ and enter into a relation to Him so intimate that it is described as an actual union. The redeeming act of Christ involved His death, burial, and resurrection. These are repeated in a spiritual sense in our salvation and are symbolized in baptism in this way:

(1) "Buried with him by baptism into death" (verse 4). Descending into the baptismal water symbolizes that we have died to sin. (2) As the water closes over our heads, it symbolizes that we lay buried with Him. This is a proof of our death to sin. This should be a real death just as His death was real. (3) "As Christ was raised up from the dead by the glory of the Father" (verse 4), so our coming out of the water should symbolize that we are now dedicated to conduct our lives as men in whom a new principle of life has been implanted.

Verse 5 teaches that we cannot be joined to Christ in one thing and not joined with Him in another. If we died out to the old nature and the old nature was crucified, the process of that death should have brought freedom to the new man in the image of Christ.

According to the *Treatise* statement a series of things are symbolized in baptism. Notice what they are: (1) The burial and resurrection of Christ. (2) The salvation of believers, including "the death of Christians to the world, the washing of their souls from the pollution of sin, their rising to newness of life." (3) The engagement of believers to serve God. (4) Their resurrection at the last day. All of these are in one way or another related to that which is symbolized in baptism.

A fact which has been assumed already is that union with Christ is not brought about by baptism but that baptism merely symbolizes what has taken place in salvation. The passage in Acts is often quoted in support of a theory of baptismal regeneration. There Peter in his message said, "Repent, and be baptized every one of you in the name of Jesus Christ for the remission of sins" (2:38). The great problem lies in the translation of the word for as rendered in the King James Version. This word has several possible renderings when translated into the English. Among these is "on the basis of." If so rendered the true meaning of the passage would be given, "Be baptized . . . on the basis of the remission of sins."

Even if this particular translation is not followed, Acts 2:38 must be interpreted in light of other Scriptures. The order is given in Acts 18:8 where it is said, "Many of the Corinthians hearing believed, and were baptized." Note the exact order: hearing, believing, baptism. This order is repeated in many other passages as well. In Philip's experience it is reported: "When they believed Philip preaching the things concerning the kingdom of God, and the name of Jesus Christ, they were baptized" (8:12). With the Ethiopian eunuch he was very plain when he requested baptism, "If thou believest with all thine heart, thou mayest" (Acts 8:37).

This same order was followed by Peter after he had preached to the family of Cornelius. After an initial experience in which they received the Holy Spirit, it was then asked, "Can any man forbid water, that these should not be bantized. which have received the Holy Ghost as well as we?" (Acts 10:47).

The example of the Philippian jailer may be taken as typical of the order followed by Paul. In that experience the jailer requested to know what he had to do to be saved. In Paul's answer, baptism is not mentioned. He and Silas simply answered, "Believe on the Lord Jesus Christ, and thou shalt be saved, and thy house" (Acts 16:31). Only later is it reported that he "was baptized, he and all his, straightway" (verse 33).

Baptism is closely related to many things in our experience, but it should be kept in mind that salvation precedes baptism. We bury only people who have died. Note, though, in the following instances the intimate relation of baptism to these things:

1. With remission of sins. In Acts 22:16 where Paul gives his testimony he relates how he was instructed to "be baptized, and wash away thy sins, calling on the name of the Lord."

2. With the new birth. Paul wrote Titus, "He saved us, by the washing of regeneration, and renewing of the Holy Ghost" (3:5).

3. With our union with Christ. To the Galatians Paul wrote, "For as many of you as have been baptized into Christ have put on Christ" (3:27).

4. With becoming a Son of God by adoption. The verse just mentioned is preceded by the verse which describes us as children of God.

5. With the bestowal of the Holy Spirit. Paul wrote, "For by one Spirit are we all baptized into one body" (1 Corinthians 12:13).

6. With our becoming a member of the church. At Pentecost it was reported: "Then they that gladly received his word were baptized: and the same day there were added unto them about three thousand souls" (Acts 2:41).

7. With the gift of salvation. Jesus is recorded by Mark to have said, "He that believeth and is baptized shall be saved" (Mark 16:16).

It may be noted that in many of these baptism is made synonymous with the work of God in the salvation experience. The interpreter should be careful to give the proper meaning. Since water baptism symbolizes the believer's identification with Christ in His burial and resurrection, the writers sometimes refer to God's act in effecting this union as baptism. But, water baptism does not bring that union into effect. It presupposes that the union has been effected and symbolizes it.

Free Will Baptists believe that immersion in water is the only biblical mode of baptism. There can be no doubt that the original form of baptism was complete immersion in water. The history of the church shows that for at least four hundred years any other form was either unknown or considered heretical. The ancient Eastern Church still rigidly adheres to immersion and counts any other mode invalid.

It is sad to say that the reformers such as Calvin did not adopt a strong stand for immersion. They even permitted infant baptism.

The Greek word *baptize* means to immerse completely. The very description of the word should be sufficient to show the mode that was practiced in the New Testament (Matthew 3:13-17). But probably the most favorable argument for immersion is found in what it symbolizes. Baptism is a symbol of the believer's identification with Christ in His burial and resurrection. There is no way that dipping, pouring, or sprinkling can be made to correspond to that. Only immersion in water gives a picture corresponding to His burial and resurrection.

As for infant baptism, the Scriptures are clear in their teaching of the fact that only those who are of age to make a specific decision of their own are candidates for baptism. Instruction (Matthew 28:19), repentance (Acts 2:38), and faith (Acts 2:41; 8:12; 18:8) are to precede baptism. The analogy of circumcision in the Old Testament is not valid. Consecration of children is all right as long as it is made evident that the consecration is of and by the parents and that the child's salvation is a private matter to be determined by his choice when he becomes of age.

II. THE LORD'S SUPPER
(Matthew 26:26-29; 1 Corinthians 11:23-30)

Three of the four gospel writers tell the story of the Lord's Supper. Paul, in First Corinthians, gives instruction about it. In both Luke 22:19 and in 1 Corinthians 11:24 instructions are given concerning its perpetuation. In the former passage Luke reports Jesus as saying, "This do in remembrance of me." Paul reported the same words in the latter passage. From Paul's words it would appear that the Lord's Supper was already established as an ordinance when Paul wrote.

The Lord's Supper was instituted on the night of our Lord's betrayal. Only John of the gospel writers does not describe the event. He does, however, refer to it and records the feet washing scene subsequent to it which was omitted by the other three. John, writing later than the others, was probably making up for their omission.

The *Treatise* states of the Lord's Supper: "This is a commemoration of the death of Christ for our sins in the use of bread which He made the emblem of His broken body, and the cup, the emblem of His shed blood, and by it the believer expresses his love for Christ, his faith and hope in Him, and pledges to Him perpetual fidelity."

The Scriptures plainly teach that the Lord's Supper symbolizes the Lord's death. Paul wrote, "For as often as ye eat this bread, and drink this cup, ye do shew the Lord's death till he come" (1 Corinthians 11:26). The death of Jesus was imminent when He initiated the supper. His death was to become the big factor in man's salvation. It was something which needed the greatest of impressions to be made upon man's mind. It was of such importance in our salvation that the Lord wanted its observance to be perpetual so that the church would constantly remind itself and the world that Christ died and why He died. The mere fact that He died would have had no significance had there been no real meaning behind His death. But there was, and the event is celebrated to show that Christ's death was necessary as an atonement for man's sin. It was also to show that His death was vicarious; it was His dying for our sins in our place.

We should note carefully the details of that first supper as described by the apostles. The supper was initiated "as they were eating" (Matthew 26:26). The Lord had sent disciples on the "first day of the feast of unleavened bread" (26:17) to prepare the place at which He would eat the passover meal with the disciples. They were all gathered in Jerusalem with thousands, and possibly millions, of Jews from all over the world. Judas had already covenanted to betray Jesus for thirty pieces of silver. But it was on the evening of the first day of this week of unleavened bread that Jesus initiated the Lord's Supper. The Supper was eaten after the regular meal had been eaten on that occasion.

In both Matthew and Mark it is recorded that Jesus first "took bread, and blessed it, and brake it, and gave it to the disciples" (Matthew 26:26; Mark 14:22), and that He then "took the cup, and gave thanks, and gave it to them" (Matthew 26:27; Mark 14:23). However, Luke records that He first "took the cup" (22:17) and "likewise also the cup after supper" (verse 20). There is no discrepancy. Apparently the single cup after the meal was the only one intended for perpetuation in the ordinance. In Jesus' words He gives no special significance to the first cup (verses 17, 18) but does to the second (verse 20).

The significance given by Jesus to the bread is simply stated in Matthew's account. He said, "Take, eat; this is my body" (26:26). Luke gives us a bit more insight into its significance when he reported that Jesus said, "This is my body which is given for you: this do in remembrance of me" (22:19). This is basically the same as Paul's report in First Corinthians 12:24. The "given for you" brings out both its vicarious aspect and its significance as an atonement for sins. This is expounded upon by Paul (Romans 3:23-25), John (1 John 4:10) and others.

More words are devoted to spelling out the significance of the cup as a symbol of the shed blood of Christ. This may be due to the fact that blood is representative life and the shedding of blood is usually made equivalent to death. Of the cup Jesus said, "This is my blood of the new testament, which is shed for many for the remission of sins" (Matthew 26:28). The words of Mark are the same as those reported by Matthew. Luke and Paul change them slightly. The words carry the significance that Jesus' shed blood of His death was the means by which the new covenant or testament was initiated. His shed blood was the basis upon which God could forgive our sins through faith in His blood.

The shed blood of Christ became a means of several things for the sinner who believes: (1) It was a means of His ransom from the power of sins (Matthew 20:28; 1 Peter 1:18). (2) It was the means by which the anger of God toward the sinner was propitiated (Romans 3:25; 1 John 2:2). (3) It was the means by which the sinner is reconciled to God (Romans 5:10; 2 Corinthians 5:18, 19; Ephesians 2:16). (4) The shed blood of Christ was accepted as a substitute for our own death, which was the penalty for our sins (Isaiah 53:6; 1 Peter 2:24; 3:18). All of these were involved then in what Jesus wished to be commemorated. It was a memorial of a life given up for us.

The Roman Catholic teaching is that the Lord's words are to be taken literally. When He said, "This is my body," He meant that the taking of the bread, and subsequently the taking of the cup, was literally partaking of the body and blood of Christ. They hold that the consecration of the elements by the priest literally changes them into the body and blood of Christ. By so doing each new consecration is a new offering of the life of Christ in sacrifice. By partaking of this new sacrifice the recipient receives saving and sanctifying grace from God. Christ is constantly sacrificed anew. This view is referred to as *transubstantiation*.

The Lutheran Church view is similar. Although they teach that the elements themselves remain unchanged, they believe that the elements are means by which the literal body and blood of Christ are communicated to the believer. By the prayer of consecration the communicant by some means actually partakes of the body and blood of Christ.

These views deny the completeness of sacrifice of Christ. That sacrifice is repeated constantly. This is in direct contradiction to the Scriptures, which teach that "by his own blood he entered in once into the holy place, having obtained eternal redemption for us" (Hebrews 9:12), and "now once in the end of the world hath he appeared to put away sin by the sacrifice of himself" (9:26). He made "one sacrifice for sins for ever" (Hebrews 10:12).

This doctrine makes the material elements necessary to the receiving of Christ and does away with spiritual reception. A system of priesthood is necesary with its external rites and ceremonies to impart Christ to all communicants. Salvation then becomes dependent upon the system rather than upon the doctrine of faith. How repugnant to the Word of God!

The bread and the cup are always presented as memorials of the body and blood of Christ. By partaking of them we do not become partakers of that death. We do this by faith. The observance of the Lord's Supper merely memorializes that death and stands as a symbol of our having partaken in His death.

The conditions of partaking in the Lord's Supper should be regeneration and a life of obedience. Closed communion, which limits the mutual observance of the Lord's Supper to the members of a particular denomination or local church, is unbiblical. The Lord gave the ordinance to His disciples who were regenerated men (Matthew 26:27). It was all believers who were present who perpetuated it in subsequent observances (Acts 2:46, 47; 20:7). Church membership is definitely not given as a prerequisite. Even baptism is not stated as a requirement, although it would generally be supposed that this initiatory rite had been observed when one was saved. However, if a church observed the Lord's Supper after one was saved and before he was baptized, there is nothing in the Scriptures to prohibit his partaking. The Supper is described by Paul as the "table of the Lord" (1 Corinthians 10:21). Paul did urge each participant to "examine himself" lest he partake of the Supper in an unworthy manner (1 Corinthians 11:27, 28). The church is not authorized to sit in judgment on any professing Christian, but we may be sure that those excluded from the church for sin (2 Thessalonians 3:6, 11; 1 Corinthians 5:11-13), for false doctrines (2 John 10, 11; Titus 3:10), and for sowing discord (Romans 16:17) were not welcomed to the Lord's table.

Jesus did not authorize any specific times to observe the Lord's Supper. The custom of the Church of Christ in observing it weekly is based on a false premise that the early church so observed it. Observance of it should be left up to the local church. This writer would advocate its observance at least annually. Our Lord simply stated, "This do in remembrance of me" (Luke 22:19). Paul said simply, "As oft as ye drink it" and "As often as ye eat this bread" (1 Corinthians 11:25, 26). It should not be observed so often that its significance becomes commonplace, but it should be observed often enough that its true significance is always strongly impressed upon the members of the body of Christ. As it expresses our hope in Him, it should always be a deep spiritual experience to all who partake.

III. WASHING THE SAINTS' FEET
(John 13:2-17)

Free Will Baptists are in the minority among the Protestant denominations who teach three ordinances instead of two. The doctrine of the washing of the saints' feet has been gradually dropped in modern times, even by many Free Will Baptists. The doctrine has a long history among Free Will Baptists and the *Treatise* contains this statement:

"This is a sacred ordinance, which teaches humility and reminds the believer of the necessity of a daily cleansing from all sin. It was instituted by the Lord Jesus Christ, and called an 'example' on the night of His betrayal, and in connection with the institution of the Lord's Supper. It is the duty and happy prerogative of every believer to observe this sacred ordinance."

The humility mentioned was aptly portrayed by our Lord when He "laid aside his garments; and took a towel, and girded himself.

171

After that he poureth water in a bason, and began to wash the disciples' feet, and to wipe them with the towel wherewith he was girded" (John 13:4, 5). He that knew "he was come from God, and went to God" had on a previous occasion declared that He came not to be ministered unto but to minister to others. That humility with which He condescended to be man and to die for man is aptly symbolized in this act. Feet washing was a servant's task, but Christ humbled Himself to do this servant's task and, thereby, set a pattern for the humility that should characterize every believer who professes to follow Him.

Baptism is the initiatory rite of the Christian by which the new believer gives evidence to the world that he has entered the new life. The Lord's Supper is that communion of saints in which they fellowship and refresh their memories of that sacrifice for their lives. Feet washing reminds us of the humility that characterized Christ and should mark each of us as a servant of others.

This ceremony also reminds us of "the necessity of a daily cleansing from sin." Simon Peter, faced with the prospect of having his Lord wash his feet, felt the need for a total cleansing by the Lord. He cried out, "Lord, not my feet only, but also my hands and my head" (John 13:9).

There have been those who argued that it is not an ordinance and that it was not initiated in relation to the Lord's Supper. A careful reading of the Scriptures will dispel this argument. It was instituted in relation to the supper from which Judas dismissed himself to betray the Lord (John 13:2-4). So was the Lord's Supper. A second argument connecting the two can be found in Peter's strong statement that he would not deny the Lord. This is found in both events (John 13:36-38; Luke 22:31-34).

Since an ordinance depends upon whether Jesus commanded it and intended it to be perpetuated or not, some have questioned it. But Jesus' statement regarding feet washing is very strong. Of the Lord's Supper, Jesus said, "This do in rememberance of me" (Luke

22:19). Of feet washing He plainly said, "Ye call me Master and Lord: and ye say well; for so I am. If I then, your Lord and Master, have washed your feet; ye also ought to wash one another's feet. For I have given you an example, that ye should do as I have done to you" (John 13:13-15). The word *ought* is used here and elsewhere to mean "to be under obligation." Jesus at no point is this emphatic in regard to the Lord's Supper. He simply gave us an example in baptism without stating it to be such. But here in specific reference to His act of humility, He said, "I have given you an example, that ye should do as I have done to you."

Probably one of the most often used arguments against feet washing is the belief that this humility may be expressed by doing a helpful deed for someone else. The substitution of this helpful deed, however, is contrary to the concept of our Lord. He said that you ought to wash feet. He gave an example of the definite act to be performed. Also it should be realized that a substitution for what Jesus commanded here would lay ground for more substitutions elsewhere. On this basis it would be all right to substitute sprinkling for baptism. It might even be taken a step further to allow substitution of church membership for regeneration. Definitely there is no basis nor authority for substitution.

The *Treatise* describes feet washing as "the duty and happy prerogative of every believer." Both duty and prerogative should be noted. Neither baptism, the Lord's Supper, nor feet washing should ever be considered duty in the sense that they are required in salvation. They are duty in the sense that our Lord commanded them and every believer should be anxious to obey the Lord in every command. They are duty also in that their observances are means by which we are witnesses to the world. But on the other hand, none of the three should be counted prerogatives in the sense that one may choose whether or not to observe them. Obedience to Christ and recognition of Him as Lord and Master make us under obligation to observe each. Feet washing is the ordinance which carries a special blessing in it. Our Lord said, "If ye know these things, happy are ye if ye do them" (John 13:17). This blessing cannot be found in denying this ordinance, but in the observance of it. So His command, His example, and His promise of a blessing should be sufficient to make every believer in Christ a feetwasher.

12

Doctrines of Last Things

BACKGROUND

Although Free Will Baptists believe that Jesus is coming again, that all will be raised from the dead, and that all will be judged, there is no complete agreement on the details surrounding these events. However, the differences of opinion should not keep Free Will Baptists from examining these truths, or from preaching them.

We should recognize that there are areas of disagreement and respect the opinions of others, whether we agree with the opinion or not. No one should be so dogmatic as to condemn those who disagree with his theories.

There is so much common ground on which Free Will Baptists can stand regarding these doctrines that it would be a shame not to emphasize our similarities rather than our differences on these subjects.

We do believe that Christ is coming. We do believe that all men will be raised from the dead. We do believe that there will be a judgment. Believing these things should cause us to be found where God would have us to be.

Several schools of thought exist regarding the Second Coming of Christ and the accompanying circumstances. One of these schools of thought is known as a-millennialism. A-millennialists believe that there will be a general resurrection of both good and bad, a general judgment, and that there is no literal thousand years of Christ's reigning on earth.

Pre-millennialists believe that Christ will come and "rapture" the saints (the dead in Christ will rise and be caught up with the living saints to meet the Lord) and that seven years later Christ will come to earth and reign on earth with His saints for a thousand years, at the end of which the wicked will be raised and judged.

Post-millennialists believe that Christianity will usher in an age of righteousness after which Christ will come, raise all the dead, and judge everyone.

There are variations within each group, but these ideas are basically what each group believes.

Many Christians would not identify with any particular group, choosing merely to believe that Christ is coming, that there will be a resurrection, and that there will be a judgment.

The main thought which should prevail in this study is to be ready, regardless of who is right.

OUTLINE

I. **Death As a Penalty of Sin (Romans 5:12-21)**

II. **Christ's Coming As the Believer's Hope (2 Thessalonians 1:5-10)**

III. **The Resurrection of the Body (1 Corinthians 15; 2 Corinthians 5:1-9)**

IV **Judgment As a Time When Probation Will Close Forever (2 Corinthians 5:10)**

INTRODUCTION

The constant emphasis of the Bible is that the present world order is not a continuing thing. It is to be replaced by another order. Whereas this order is material and will pass away, that new order which will come will be spiritual and eternal. Probably the first hint of this came with the introduction of death into this order. The life of man on earth was seen to be temporal and passing; however, there was seen to be an eternal quality in the soul of man. With the recognition that God was an eternal being and the revelation that man was created in His image and likeness, there grew a sense of eternity that led to hope for a future life.

The climax of the Old Testament teaching on the subject probably came in the testimony of Job. His witness was: "I know that my redeemer liveth, and that he shall stand at the latter day upon the earth: And though after my skin worms destroy this body, yet in my flesh shall I see God" (19:25, 26). The climax of the hope of the ages comes in the New Testament in the resurrection of Christ. His resurrection gave witness to His testimony that He was the Son of God and that His claims were true. He witnessed to the fact that there was an eternity in the future, consisting of a spiritual realm in which the saints of God would bask forever in the light of God's presence.

The doctrines gleaned from both testaments dealing with last things is referred to as eschatology. This term is based on the biblical references to "the last days," "the end times," and other similar references. Death is included in these studies because of its vital relation to them.

I. DEATH AS A PENALTY OF SIN
(Romans 5:12-21)

Physical death is not represented in the Scriptures as an expected natural result of man's original condition. Created in the image of God, had those inherent spiritual potentials been realized, death and mortality would not have been man's end. But when man sinned and died spiritually, death was introduced into the world by humanity. This is that of which Paul wrote when he said, "Wherefore, as by one man sin entered into the world, and death by sin; and so death passed upon all men, for that all have sinned" (Romans 5:12). So death was foreign and hostile to God's intent for man.

The *Treatise* statement is in accord with this view. It states that "As a result of sin, all mankind is subject to the death of the body."

Actually, two scriptural thoughts are involved in this statement: (1) Death was introduced because of sin; and (2) death was universal in that all men became subject to it. The second is a natural result of the first since "All have sinned, and come short of the glory of God."

The fact that needs positive emphasis is that death was introduced as a punishment for sin. God's decree had been to man, "Of the fruit of the tree which is in the midst of the garden . . . Ye shall not eat of it, neither shall ye touch it, lest ye die" (Genesis 3:3). Man's disobedience was a deliberative act with knowledge of the consequences. It was "by one man" that sin, and death as a result of sin, entered into the world. But that death has "passed upon all men" because all men since have followed in the steps of Adam and have sinned.

This view stands in contrast to the liberal thought of modern commentators. Representative of these is C. H. Dodd who in his commentary of the book of Romans said of Paul's concept: "Obviously we cannot accept such a speculation as an account of the origin of death, which is a natural process inseparable from organic existence in the world we know, and devoid of any moral significance." Such refutations of Paul's argument stand against the teachings of the Word of God and ignore the divine influence in the production of the Scriptures. The origin of death unquestionably is linked to sin by God's Word and it does have a deep moral significance. Any view other than this denies the teaching of the inspired Word of God.

Another fallacy that must be avoided is that Adam's sin only affected man as a bad example. This teaching says that Adam was an outstanding representative man and that he influenced many for bad. It also teaches that Jesus was an outstanding representative man with the opposite influence. Both have perpetuated their influence through great periods of civilization. Actually, there is much more involved than this. Adam's sin did more than just create an example for other men, and Jesus did more than just set a moral example for man. As the *Treatise* states, "In consequence of the first transgression, the state under which the posterity of Adam came into the world is so different from that of Adam that they have not that righteousness and purity which Adam had before the fall; they are not willing to obey God, but are inclined to evil." The influence of Christ has no effect upon man except as a man accepts "the redemption effected through the blood of Christ."

There are certain natural consequences that are a part of the penalty of sin. But the full penalty is of a specific nature described well in the Word of God. The one word which describes that penalty upon sin is death. That death is an expression of the holy wrath of God upon the sinner.

Death must be described according to its threefold aspect:

1. Physical death is the separation of soul and body and marks the stop of man's earthly life. The body may be preserved to some extent, but it is devoid of life. This is the death described in Genesis 3:19 where it is recorded, "In the sweat of thy face shalt thou eat bread, till thou return unto the ground; for out of it wast thou taken: for dust thou art, and unto dust shalt thou return." This is death that is described in the constantly recurring refrain in chapter 5 of Genesis: "And he died" (verses 5, 8, 11, 14, 17, etc.).

The penal character of this death has been removed for the believer, for Christ has endured death as the penalty of our sin. Death to the believer is merely the gateway through which he enters his eternal existence. "To be absent from the body" is but "to be present with the Lord" (2 Corinthians 5:8). With Paul we can say, "To die is gain" (Philippians 1:21).

2. Spiritual death is the separation of the soul from God. Physical death is of little consequence in contrast with spiritual death. The penalty announced by God in Eden was primarily the death of the soul (Genesis 2:17; 3:3). It may be that Paul was speaking chiefly of this aspect of death when he wrote, "That as sin hath reigned unto death, even so might grace reign through righteousness unto eternal life by Jesus Christ our Lord" (Romans 5:21). Man spiritually dead can be reborn and find life in Jesus Christ. This is the death of which Jesus spoke to Nicodemus when He said, "Ye must be born again" (John 3:7).

It was by death that man lost the presence and favor of God. As Jesus said, "God is a Spirit: and they that worship him must worship him in spirit and in truth" (John 4:24). Man spiritually dead has no knowledge and desire for God. Only by a resurrection to a new life, a spiritual quickening, can he have restored favor in the presence of God.

3. Eternal death is the completion and culmination of spiritual death. The man who remains unreborn spiritually at death enters a state of eternal death. At physical death the sinner enters a condition of eternal separation from God. This state is filled with remorse and terrible outward punishments according to the Word of God. Jesus described the place of eternal death as one of "everlasting fire" (Matthew 25:41). Paul called it "everlasting destruction from the presence of the Lord, and from the glory of his power" (2 Thessalonians 1:9). It is then eternal and a condition beyond remedy.

Many questions have been asked about the state of man between physical death and the time he enters his eternal reward in either Heaven or Hell. It is evident that the soul does not cease to exist. From the Scriptures it appears that the soul of the righteous, or the one reborn spiritually, enters into a state of blessedness and happiness. No better illustration can be given than that described for Lazarus in the story of the rich man and Lazarus. The place where Lazarus rested on the bosom of Abraham stood in stark contrast to the abode of the rich man. Lazarus was in ideal conditions and had no need.

The soul of the wicked, the one dead in trespasses and sins, will enter into a state of misery. This wretched condition is given illustration in the situation in which the rich man existed. It is a place of torment and unrest and partakes somewhat of the eternal state into which the wicked will enter after judgment.

There is no purgatory or neutral condition in which the condition of the soul is undetermined. The condition in which death finds a soul is the condition in which the soul will enter eternity and remain forever. There is no probation or second chance. Prayers for the soul of the dead will not avail to change their condition.

Two other false doctrines are rejected by Free Will Baptists. One is the doctrine which believes that in death the soul becomes unconscious or asleep at death and remains in that slumbering condition until the resurrection. The second one teaches annihilation, which hold that the soul of the wicked man will be destroyed by the fires of judgment and cease to exist. We believe that the soul of every man will exist eternally in either Hell or Heaven following the judgment.

II. CHRIST'S COMING AS THE BELIEVER'S HOPE
(2 Thessalonians 1:5-10)

The Second Coming of Christ is the "blessed hope" of the believer. It is set to be the key event in the end time and the finish of time. Although liberalism has interpreted this event as something other than a literal, visible return, to Free Will Baptists it remains one of the fundamental truths of the faith.

This doctrine is important enough in the Holy Scriptures to be mentioned in at least one out of every thirty verses. For every mention of the first coming of Christ there are eight references to His Second Coming. Long passages in the teachings of Christ and other writings in the New Testament refer to it. In fact, the whole of First and Second Thessalonians is devoted to the subject of the Second Coming. This is not to mention the relation it has to the whole book of Revelation.

The passage in 2 Thessalonians 1:5-10 is typical of those which refer to the Second Coming. In this passage Paul points out some of the key things which will be related to the coming of Christ.

1. "The Lord Jesus shall be revealed from heaven" (verse 7). There is no question but that Paul believed that Jesus was literally coming again. He had surely heard from the apostles and believed the words of the angels at the ascension of Christ who said, "This same Jesus, which is taken up from you into heaven, shall so come in like manner as ye have seen him go into heaven" (Acts 1:11). Jesus Himself had given testimony to His return when He said, "I go to prepare a place for you. And if I go and prepare a place for you, I will come again, and receive you unto myself; that where I am, there ye may be also" (John 14:2, 3).

2. Jesus shall be accompanied "with his mighty angels." The hosts of Heaven will accompany the victorious Christ on His return. They will have a specific purpose in being with Him. Speaking of this time Jesus had said, "The Son of man shall send

forth his angels, and they shall gather out of his kingdom all things that offend, and them which do iniquity; and shall cast them into a furnace of fire" (Matthew 13:41, 42). Jesus also said, "So shall it be at the end of the world: the angels shall come forth, and sever the wicked from among the just" (Matthew 13:49).

3. Jesus shall take "vengeance on them that know not God" and shall punish them "with everlasting destruction from the presence of the Lord." The question of judgment on the unrighteous will be further dealt with later, but it is important to state here that it is an event vitally related to the Second Coming. The suffering of saints suggests that there will be a time of recompense of evil upon the unrighteous. That day when all things will be made right will follow the Second Coming.

4. Jesus shall "be glorified in his saints." Believers are each destined to be "a partaker of the glory that shall be revealed" (1 Peter 5:1). We are told that the God of all grace "hath called us unto his eternal glory by Christ Jesus" (5:10). The ultimate purpose of God was to display His glory. The climax then of all creation will come when saints shall share as joint heirs with Christ in that Heaven which will display the full glory of God.

The *Free Will Baptist Treatise* statement contains basically what these verses from Paul has in them. That statement reads: "The Lord Jesus, who ascended on high and sits at the right hand of God, will come again to close the Gospel dispensation, glorify His saints, and judge the world." These words express a belief in the literal personal, bodily return of Christ. They stand in contrast to the beliefs of those who interpret the Second Coming to refer to something else. Some things which have been used as the second coming of Christ are (1) the coming of the Holy Spirit, (2) the coming of Christ into a life at salvation, (3) the death of a saint when he goes to be with Christ, or (4) the conversion of the world.

Paul's teachings about a literal return of Christ are plain. He wrote to the Thessalonians that "the Lord himself shall descend from heaven with a shout, with the voice of the archangel, and with the trump of God: and the dead in Christ shall rise first: Then we which are alive and remain shall be caught up together with them in the clouds, to meet the Lord in the air" (1 Thessalonians 4:16, 17). He speaks of "the coming of our Lord Jesus Christ" (5:23) as something which could not be fulfilled without the person of Christ. He mentions how the saints of God "wait for his Son from heaven" (1:10; 3:13; 4:16).

The writers of the other books of the New Testament agree with Paul's view. James' statement cannot be interpreted otherwise than as a personal coming (5:7, 8). Peter ran into scoffers in his day who asked, "Where is the promise of his coming?" (2 Peter 3:4). He described that coming in very specific terms: "The day of the Lord will come as a thief in the night" (3:10). He went on to describe the terrors of that day. In his first epistle, he wrote, "When the chief Shepherd shall appear, ye shall receive a crown of glory that fadeth not away" (1 Peter 5:4). John expected it to be a personal return else he would not have exhorted believers to "abide in him; that, when he shall appear, we may have confidence, and not be ashamed before him at his coming" (1 John 2:28). Jude, too, must have believed in a literal return. Quoting Enoch he wrote: "Behold, the Lord cometh with ten thousands of his saints" (verse 14).

The return of Christ "will close the Gospel dispensation." Many writers have attempted to set forth their views of the sequence of events in the end time. Elaborate schemes, supposedly based on Scriptures, have been outlined and many of them are very impressive. The multiplicity of views regarding the events surrounding the Second Coming has led to sharp clashes in some circles. Free Will Baptists generally may be classified as a-millennialists or pre-millennialists in their beliefs of the doctrines of the last things. The a-millennialists do not believe in a literal reign of Christ during a thousand year period on earth. The pre-millennialists believe that Christ will reign on earth for a thousand years in a near ideal kingdom in which the Jews will come forth as a believing force.

Regardless of the particular events related to the Second Coming, on the basic questions Free Will Baptists are in close harmony. The denomination teaches that the coming of Christ is imminent. There is no time given by the Scriptures which would tell us the date of this event. It is declared to be beyond the knowledge of men and angels (Matthew 24:36). The revealed Word does mention that there will be signs which will point to the nearness of that return. Apostasy and departure from the faith will precede that event (1 Timothy 4:1; 2 Timothy 3:1-5). In fact, Paul remarked that "that day shall not come, except there come a falling away first" (2 Thessalonians 2:3). Jesus indicated that a widespread preaching of the gospel in all the world would be one sign of the return of Christ (Matthew 24:14).

In the present situation there appears to be nothing that would prevent the sudden and immediate return of Christ to the earth. Jesus meant for every believer of every age to anticipate His return at any moment. Paul and the other early church fathers were not in error in believing that Christ might return in their lifetimes. It seems that the Lord gave the promise of His coming and left the timing of it indefinite for a purpose. Believers are never to relax their pilgrim hearts for "in such an hour as ye think not the Son of man cometh" (Matthew 24:44). The admonition for every believer is given in these words of Jesus: "Watch therefore, for ye know neither the day nor the hour wherein the Son of man cometh" (Matthew 25:13).

Peter used the imminent return of the Lord as an incentive to holy living. He wrote of the Second Coming and then said to his readers, "Wherefore, beloved, seeing that ye look for such things, be diligent that ye may be found of him in peace, without spot, and blameless" (2 Peter 3:14).

On the following points almost all Free Will Baptists would agree: (1) Jesus is literally coming again as He went away. (2) His coming can be at any moment. There is nothing that any of us could adjudge as barring an immediate, sudden return. (3) Believers should maintain expectant hearts. Belief in His imminent return should encourage us to keep our hearts pure. This thought should drive us to evangelism and a deep desire to win the lost before it is too late. (4) When Jesus comes, He will judge the world. Every man will be judged and given his due according to his past response to God and His Word. The saints will be glorified and ushered into an eternal abode with Christ. The ones judged unworthy will be cast into outer darkness where there will be weeping, wailing, and gnashing of teeth.

III. THE RESURRECTION OF THE BODY
(1 Corinthians 15; 2 Corinthians 5:1-9)

The great truths of the Bible generally have at least one section of the Scriptures devoted almost exclusively to each of them. When the resurrection is mentioned, every Bible student immediately thinks of 1 Corinthians 15. It is in this passage that Paul gives a broad discussion of that topic. At no other place is such broad coverage given to the resurrection.

The doctrine of the resurrection of men depends upon the truth of the resurrection of Christ. In fact, all of the doctrines of Christianity hinge upon this key fact of Christian truth. Even in Paul's day there were those who cast slander on the doctrine. Paul, too, argued that "if Christ be not risen, then is our preaching vain, and your faith is also vain" (1 Corinthians 15:14). We cannot agree with the modern church men who have only a human Christ and whose only hope is in a dead man. As Paul wrote, "If in this life only we have hope in Christ, we are of all men most miserable" (verse 19).

The *Treatise* statement on the future resurrection says: "The Scriptures teach the resurrection of the bodies of all men, each in its own order; they that have done good will come forth to the resurrection of life, and they that have done evil to the resurrection of damnation."

All men must die. The human body because of sin was made subject to death. But the Scriptures specifically teach that death is not the end. Man will be resurrected bodily in the end time.

Although we believe that the bodies of men will be resurrected, this is not necessarily to argue that man will come forth with the exact body he possessed at death. For the believer Paul taught that God will "fashion anew the body of our humiliation, that it may be conformed to the body of his glory" (Philippians 3:21 ASV). Although there is some connection, Paul taught that "thou sowest not that body that shall be" (1 Corinthians 15:37). He went on to explain that "It is sown in corruption; it is raised in incorruption: it is sown in dishonour; it is raised in glory: it is sown in weakness; it is raised in power: it is sown a natural body; it is raised a spiritual body" (verses 42-44). So he describes it as incorruptible, glorious, powerful, and spiritual in contrast to the natural human body that we now bear. In verse 49 he says that "we shall also bear the image of the heavenly." This is the one that will conform to "his glorious body" (Philippians 3:21).

Some have pressed the view that our body will be like the post-resurrection body of Christ. The body of the believer will surely resemble that body of Christ but not in every detail. His appearances were to human eyes, and some details of His appearances may have been just for the benefit of His earthly audience. When we receive our new bodies, they will not be subjects of earthly eyes but spiritual ones only.

The believer's body will not be flesh and blood (verse 50). Although it will be a spiritual body, it will be no less real than our natural body. It will no longer have human tendencies and will be in every way adaptable to heavenly surroundings (verse 44). No longer subject to death, it will be in complete accord with its heavenly abode.

The Scriptures do not give as much insight into the nature of the body of the unbeliever as it does of the believer. The Scriptures do teach that the bodies of the wicked will be raised. Jesus said, "The hour is coming, in the which all that are in the graves shall hear his voice, And shall come forth; they that have done good, unto the resurrection of life; and they that have done evil, unto the resurrection of damnation" (John 5:28, 29). Paul taught that "there shall be a resurrection of the dead, both of the just and unjust" (Acts 24:15).

The bodies of the wicked will surely be different from that of the believer. The body of the believer will necessarily be adaptable to his spiritual and heavenly surroundings. The body of the wicked will be that which would correspond to the "resurrection of damnation." Since they "shall have their part in the lake which burneth with fire and brimstone" (Revelation 21:8), their bodies must be fitted for such an abode. This "second death" is described by Jesus as a destruction of body and soul but it is an everlasting destruction (Matthew 10:28). Since this is eternal death (just as the believer has eternal life), it must involve an eternal dying and all of the horrors accompanying death and banishment from the presence of God.

The chief point of the doctrine of the resurrection is that death does not end man's existence. Of course, this doctrine is in accord with all the teachings of the Word of God. God created man with never dying qualities and appointed him an eternal existence in ideal conditions. Though man sinned and lost hope in that eternal existence, hope has been restored through Jesus Christ. Through the reconciliation effected by the shed blood of Christ, man can be restored to hope of eternal life. Jesus conquered death for man, and death holds no valid claim on man. As Christ was raised, so we too can share in the resurrection by faith in Christ.

IV. JUDGMENT AS A TIME WHEN PROBATION WILL CLOSE FOREVER
(2 Corinthians 5:10)

Closely related to the doctrines of death, resurrection, and the Second Coming is the doctrine of judgment. The Bible is filled with this ever recurring subject. The doctrine of judgment as revealed in the Word of God gives man a definite understanding of that which his conscience testifies to him. In every age of man history shows that the human race has believed in a time when there would be judgment and retribution upon the evil deeds of men. The hearts and consciences of men seem universally to look forward to judgment.

The *Treatise* states: "There will be a judgment, when time and man's probation will close forever. Then all men will be judged according to their works." Although Free Will Baptists differ in their interpretations of this statement, all are agreed with the two basic facts in it: (1) there will be a judgment for every one; (2) all will be judged.

The writer of the book of Ecclesiastes wrote: "For God shall bring every work into judgment, with every secret thing, whether it be good, or whether it be evil" (12:14). This was his conclusion after investigating all the ways of man. He, too, was teaching two main facts: There will be judgment; men both evil and good will be judged.

The book of Job was probably written to explain the seeming unfairness of life. The evil men prospered while the righteous men often suffered and had no proper retribution for their goodness in this life. It was through his sufferings that he came to realize that some day a Redeemer would plead his cause and help settle the lack of equality of justice of this life (Job 9:32; 19:25).

189

The psalmist also recognized that there would be a future judgment when God would intervene and bring man to account for his deeds. He wrote: "For he cometh, for he cometh to judge the earth: he shall judge the world with righteousness, and the people with his truth" (96:13). And again there are two facts that predominate: (1) there will be a judgment, and (2) "the earth" and "the people" shall be universally judged.

The New Testament is filled with references on judgment. Paul, in his message to the Athenians, said, "He hath appointed a day, in the which he will judge the world in righteousness by that man whom he hath ordained" (Acts 17:31). To the two facts which stand out in the previous passages, a new item is added. This is that the judge will be by "that man whom he hath ordained." Paul mentioned elsewhere about "the day when God shall judge the secrets of men by Jesus Christ" (Romans 2:16). Jesus Himself had revealed that "the Father judgeth no man, but hath committed all judgment unto the Son" (John 5:22).

The *Treatise* statement says that "all men will be judged according to their works." John in Revelation gives a brief glimpse into a judgment scene. He wrote: "I saw the dead, small and great, stand before God; and the books were opened: and another book was opened, which is the book of life: and the dead were judged out of those things which were written in the books, according to their works" (20:12). The "works" here would surely mean conformity to the teachings of Jesus and the conditions of salvation. This concept is repeated in many places. For example, Paul introduced it in his letter to the Corinthians. He said, "For we must all appear before the judgment seat of Christ; that everyone may receive the things done in his body, according to that he hath done, whether it be good or bad" (2 Corinthians 5:10).

The severity of the judgment is stressed in many Scriptures. False professors that have even done mighty works in His name will be told, "Depart from me, ye that work iniquity" (Matthew

7:23). The ones represented as goats on His left hand in the great judgment scene will hear this pronouncement: "Depart from me, ye cursed, into everlasting fire, prepared for the devil and his angels" (Matthew 25:41).

A man's works will not be just those outward expressions of his life which we see. The secrets of every man's heart and soul will be taken into account. The Judge will take note of the most inward elements of each life: the impulses, the motives, the thoughts. It will be much more strict than most men expect. Jesus said that account must be given even of idle words (Matthew 12:36).

The believer in Christ must face judgment, but judgment for him should hold no fear. It is the heart of the unsaved which should be concerned. Judgment will only open the woeful eternity for him.

Chapter Twelve

13

Our Church Covenant

BACKGROUND

A covenant is an agreement which has been entered into between two people, between one person and several persons, between one or more persons and God, or a mutual agreement among several persons.

There is nothing new in the Covenant idea, the history of such dating back to primitive peoples. Many curious methods of adopting a covenant are known from history.

Church groups besides Free Will Baptists have their covenants, some of which are quite similar to ours. We are not peculiar, therefore, as far as having a Church Covenant is concerned. Rather, it would be strange if we did not have one.

The *Treatise* states that those who wish to become members of our churches are, among other things, to adopt our Covenant. Yet, how many Free Will Baptists are really familiar with the Covenant?

Our Covenant contains many outstanding promises which would reflect a greater support of God's worldwide program if every Free Will Baptist faithfully kept them. There are many areas of the Christian life which are covered by the Covenant, areas that are too often neglected.

A study of the Covenant such as is presented in this lesson should be an effective way of reminding all of us of our obligation to God and to each other.

An interesting resolution was adopted by the Thirtieth General Conference of Free Will Baptists at Sutton, Vermont, October 6, 1847, and reads as follows:

"Whereas there exists in the denomination a difference of opinion, in relation to the propriety of using written covenants in our churches, and the establishment of our Biblical School,— Therefore, Resolved, That such a difference of opinion ought not create a breach of Christian or church fellowship, but brethren, who may differ in their views on these points, should exercise mutual forbearance, and endeavor to express their views with candor, Christian kindness and courtesy."

It is difficult to see why anyone would object to our Covenant.

OUTLINE

   I. The Gift of Ourselves (1 Thessalonians 1:1-7)
  II. Abstinence From Sinful Practices (1 Thessalomans 1:8-10)
 III. The Pledge to Sanctification (Philippians 1:1-7)
  IV. The Support of the Church (2 Corinthians 11:7-11)
   V The Watchcare Over Believers (Galatians 6:1-10)
  VI. The Extension of the Kingdom (Colossians 1:1-8)
 VII. The Support of Denominational Enterprises (Philippians 4:2; Romans 16:1, 2; Titus 3:13)

INTRODUCTION

This lesson is a study of the Free Will Baptist Church Covenant. This is a very neglected item in many of our churches. Many members have been taken into the church without realizing its existence. Sad to say, many members have never "taken" the Covenant, although they are supposedly bound to it with the other members of the church. The taking of this Covenant should solemnize the entrance of every new believer into church membership. It should be read regularly to keep all members aware of their solemn obligations to each other, to the church, and chiefly to Christ.

A covenant is a mutual compact between two or more parties. Usually it binds the individual parties to fulfill certain conditions and promises certain advantages to each party. A covenant is not a creed. A creed is a statement of belief and pledge to those beliefs, which distinguishes those who take it from others. The Free Will Baptist Church Covenant was not intended to set forth doctrine, but its conditions and pledges do set forth beliefs, which distinguish Free Will Baptists from those who do not hold these principles. Loyalty to this covenant will make one a faithful servant of the principles of Christ.

I. THE GIFT OF OURSELVES
(1 Thessalonians 1:1-7)

Paul commended the Macedonians of whom he testified that they "first gave their own selves to the Lord, and unto us by the will of God" (2 Corinthians 8:5). That commendation by Paul probably served our fathers as an example when they wrote this preamble to our Church Covenant. This preamble is in accord with the Word of God in other ways as well. For one thing, it maintains the proper order of placing our devotion. God is always first in demand of our lives and devotion. Others follow Him. However, it is important to have both in our outlook. Love God and love your neighbor was Jesus' concept of fulfilling the commandments of God. And John taught us, "If a man say, I love God, and hateth his brother, he is a liar: for he that loveth not his brother whom he hath seen, how can he love God whom he hath not seen?" (1 John 4:20).

It is also in accord with the Word of God in that it works for the unity of the body of Christ. Jesus prayed for us, "That they all may be one" (John 17:21). It is the will of God that we be bound in a spiritual unity. This Covenant is an outward token of that spiritual unity which we feel because we are united in Him.

The two bases for this Covenant are mentioned in this preamble. They are (1) "faith in Christ" and (2) the adoption of "the Word of God as our rule of faith and practice." Free Will Baptists share a common faith in Christ. Evidence of faith in Christ is the only prerequisite for membership in our church. But we believe in a living, vital faith that appropriates the grace of God and is expressed through a changed life.

Accepting the Word of God as our rule of faith and practice also binds Free Will Baptists to one another. To us the Word of God is sacred because it contains the revelation of God to man concerning what he needs to know about God, how to be saved, and how to go to Heaven. Nothing supersedes the Word of God as an authority for faith and practice. The Christian Science religion looks to *Key To The Holy Scriptures* by Mary Baker Eddy. The Mormons look to the *Book of Mormon*. The Catholics have the authority of the clergy which supersedes the Word of God. But to Free Will Baptists the Bible is "a sufficient and infallible rule and guide to salvation and all Christian worship and service."

This passage in 1 Thessalonians 1:1-7 gives an insight into the closeness of the Christian fellowship. Paul, Silas, and Timothy were evangelists for Christ, but they thanked God for the churches (verse 2) and were always praying for them. They remembered their "work of faith, and labour of love, and patience of hope" as it related to their work. Their being bound together is seen in the fact that Paul told the Thessalonian believers that "ye became followers of us" (verse 6) and "ye were ensamples to all that believe in

Macedonia and Achaia" (verse 7). Paul elsewhere mentions the term "from faith to faith." This exemplifies what Paul is talking about here. These evangelists believed and carried the Word to Thessalonica. The Thessalonians believed and became examples to others in their country. Thus lives became intertwined as faith was spread from one heart to another. Because of this dependence on one another, we need to give ourselves constantly to each other for mutual growth in the faith.

The Covenant is solemn because of its gravity. It is important that believers be aware of their obligations to God and to each other. This Covenant makes public those ties and obligations which bind us to each other and gives us a basis for further service.

II. ABSTINENCE FROM SINFUL PRACTICES
(1 Thessalomans 1:8-10)

There are four promises made in the second paragraph. These are: (1) to love and obey Him in all things; (2) to avoid all apearance of evil; (3) to abstan from all sinful amusements and unholy conformity to the world and all sanction of the use and sale of intoxicating beverages; and (4) to "provide things honest in the sight of all men."

Notice that there are two positive and two negative statements involved in this: to love and obey Him and to be honest are the positive ones; to avoid appearances of evil and to abstain from particular evils make up the negative ones. Each of these in a significant way will contribute to the accomplishment of abstinence from sinful practices.

"To love and obey Him in all things" is but to keep the first and greatest of the commandments. From the beginning this has been revealed as God's plan for man. It was because of a failure to obey God that sin came first upon the human race. When God later gave the preface to the law which He revealed to Moses, He said, "If ye will obey my voice indeed, and keep my covenant, then ye shall be a peculiar treasure unto me above all people" (Exodus 19:5). It was Solomon who later wrote, "Fear God, and keep his commandments for this is the whole duty of man" (Ecclesiastes 12:13).

If the believer loves God, that love is going to lead to a life of positive action for Christ and an avoidance of particular sins. In the passage of Scripture given for this section, Paul mentioned to the Thessalonians "how ye turned to God from idols to serve the living and true God" (1 Thessalonians 1:9). Turning to God involves in the person who turns a decision that God is worthy above all gods to merit His trust. It requires in the person an acceptance of the revelation which God has given in His Word. A decision to turn to God requires that one love God and the natural result of love should be obedience.

That they turned "from idols" would suggest a turning from evil. Idolatry generally involves moral evil. Even the religious rites and ceremonies involve practices which would have to be shunned by believers. The Jerusalem Council in dealing with the problem of converts who turned from idols urged the new believers to "abstain from meats offered to idols, and from blood, and from things strangled, and from fornication" (Acts 15:29). These were things which bore an appearance of evil. The apostles knew that identification with these things would mark the believer as being like the world so they were urged to avoid them.

James, in his description of undefiled and pure religion, urged the believer to "keep himself unspotted from the world" (1:27). If the believer associates himself with evil, he will become "spotted." The old saying was, "If you run with the dogs, you'll get fleas." So it is with worldliness. The believer has to avoid the very appearance of evil or he will tarnish his reputation as a Christian.

What is considered "sinful amusements" has gone through many changes in recent years. Actually young people are often perplexed as they look for guidelines in amusements. A sinful amusement would be any recreation or pleasure which involved bad morals, indecency, dishonor to the cause of Christ, or a conflict with spiritual values. Paul gives two principles by which to guide believers: (1) "Let no man seek his own, but every man another's wealth" (1 Corinthians 10:24). Whatever would hinder others should be omitted. One cannot afford to break the conscience of others. (2) "Whether therefore ye eat, or drink, or whatsoever ye do, do all to the glory of God" (verse 31). If anything will not honor God or the believer as a servant of God, it should be omitted from one's life.

Paul was very definite in denouncing "unholy conformity to the world." He wrote, "Ye cannot drink the cup of the Lord, and the cup of devils" (1 Corinthians 10:21). There is such a distinction between the two that partaking with either marks us for what we really are.

One of the things against which Free Will Baptists take a specific stand is "the use and sale of intoxicating beverages." In a day of diminishing conviction in regard to the drinking of alcoholic beverages and the influences of drug addiction we still insist that it is better to "be filled with the Spirit" and influenced by Him than to be filled with those elements which cause us to lose control of our wills and result in excesses which are not becoming to the believer.

The believer is "to provide things honest in the sight of all men." The business, political, and social world is constantly rocked by revelations of great dishonesty. It even reaches into the religious world. But honesty is the mark of a true Christian. Because of his adherence to truth and what is right, he must be honest with all men and with himself. While others are cheating on income tax and padding expense accounts, he finds it necessary to be true to himself. Complete honesty in word, finance, and deed will commend the believer's testimony to all men.

III. THE PLEDGE TO SANCTIFICATION
(Phiippians 1:1-7)

The third paragraph of the Covenant deals with a pledge to Christian growth. It covers the obligations of believers in (1) the study of the Scriptures, (2) prayer, both personal and family, and (3) worship. It also includes other obligations which result in growth in the Christian experience.

Paul refers to believers as "saints" in various passages (Philippians 1:1). A saint is a holy person or one who has been sanctified. Believers may be referred to as saints because the holiness of God has been imputed to them. But, although they are saints positionally and separated unto God, their growth in grace or continuing sanctification is God's will. This is why Paul continues in the Philippian letter to say, "Being confident of this very thing, that he which hath begun a good work in you will perform it until the day of Jesus Christ" (1:6). God is ever working in the believer to bring him to spiritual maturity.

The means of this growth on the part of the believer will always be the study of the Scriptures, prayer, and worship. It is through the Scriptures that the Lord continuously speaks to believers. The Bible is the record of God's progressive revelation of Himself to man. It is important for each believer to know what God has revealed about Himself, our salvation, and eternity. There are no other means by which man can learn of these things. This is why Jesus insisted: "Search the scriptures; for in them ye think ye have eternal life: and they are they which testify of me" (John 5:39). This is why the psalmist of the Old Testament rejoiced in the Word of the Lord, because it revealed God's law and will to him (Psalm 119).

God speaks to man through the Word of God and man communes with God through prayer. Both private prayer and community prayer are important. Jesus urged private prayers. He said, "When thou prayest, enter into thy closet, and when thou hast shut thy door, pray to thy Father which is in secret; and thy Father which seeth in secret shall reward thee openly" (Matthew 6:6). It is prayer of this nature which loses all of its pretense. If we are not careful, public prayer will become more of an object for man to hear than for God to hear. This is not good. But every believer should develop a constant, everyday, personal prayer life. This is why Paul encouraged believers to "pray without ceasing" (1 Thessalonians 5:17).

Family devotions should be developed in every believer's home. Family devotions should contain both prayer and Bible reading. It should be a daily time of worship, which supplements the weekly worship services of the family at church. Parents who expect their children to become followers of Christ can effectively use this time for instruction and training.

The writer of Hebrews gave us an admonition that will stand always. He urged believers to forsake not "the assembling of ourselves together, as the manner of some is; but exhorting one another: and so much the more, as ye see the day approaching" (Hebrews 10:25). He recognized the need for social worship. Common admonition and joint worship are always strengthening to the believer. Man is a social creature, and union in worship brings the body of Christ together in a way that nothing else will. Decline in attendance to the house of the Lord is usually accompanied by a decline in one's spiritual life. When the psalmist said, "Let the redeemed of the LORD say so" (Psalm 107:2), he must have been referring to the joyful testimony of believers engaged in worship.

Sanctification will result as the believer "by self-denial, faith, and good works" endeavors to grow. The walk of a saint is one of self-denial as in Jesus' day and all times, the spiritual way is one that calls for self-sacrifice. When Jesus invited followers, did He not say, "If any man will come after me, let him deny himself, and take up his cross, and follow me" (Matthew 16:24)?

Peter wrote his second epistle to tell how to grow in grace and knowledge of Christ. In the first chapter he tells us how that faith is only the beginning and that we grow by adding other Christian virtues to our beginning faith. It is James who teaches us the proper relation of good works to faith. It is through good works that we express our faith. By doing good works we become aware that the principles of Christ are active in us.

IV. THE SUPPORT OF THE CHURCH
(2 Corinthians 11:7-11)

What is the obligation of the believer to the church? Such a question cannot be answered by attending one, two, or even three services of the week. Attendance at the service is no real mark of one's dedication to Christ. The church is the means by which Christ ordained that we should express our Christian experience and witness to the lost about Him. When one falls in love with Christ, dedication to the activities of the church should naturally result.

One of the best ways to begin our support of the church is by our presence. The believer should attend all phases of the church services. This would include Sunday school, Church Training Service, worship services, prayer meetings, and even church conferences. Each of these auxiliaries has been set up under the leadership of the Holy Spirit to make a distinct contribution to each believer's life. The complete Christian will feel an obligation to each one.

The Free Will Baptist Covenant urges the "observances of the ordinances." Some churches teach that these are essential to salvation or are means of imparting grace to the believer. We believe that they are the duty and privilege of the believer. They are strengthening to him as they bring him to a greater knowledge of what they symbolize. No believer can practice them without becoming more aware of their significance. What Jesus said of feet washing might be said of all the ordinances: "If ye know these things, happy are ye if ye do them" (John 13:17).

The duty and obligation of observing the ordinances should never be minimized. Although we might not term them as "essential to salvation," we must recognize that they are essential to obedience to our Lord Jesus Christ. It is not so much that they commend us to God but the fact that their observance brings a blessing to the heart of the one who obeys. And as we "shew forth his death," we give a witness to the world around us that we love Him and are His obedient servants.

Our Covenant pledges each member "to pay according to our ability for the support of the church, of its poor, and all its benevolent work." In our *Articles of Faith* it is stated that we believe the following about tithing: "God commanded tithes and offerings in the Old Testament; Jesus Christ endorsed it in the Gospel (Matthew 23:23), and the Apostle Paul said, 'Upon the first day of the week let every one of you lay by him in store, as God hath prospered him' (1 Corinthians 16:2a)." The most equitable and simple way to support the church is tithing. Tithing fulfills the "according to our ability" clause of the Covenant.

Of course, tithing should be a minimum amount to give. The person with fewer obligations and a greater income should be a generous steward of that with which God has blessed him. We are not stewards of ten percent of our income but of the one hundred percent. Where ability allows one to do so, a person should dedicate all that he can to the service of Christ.

But giving should sometimes be "above one's ability" or sacrificially. Paul commended the Macedonians for such a gift. He wrote

"How that in a great trial of affliction the abundance of their joy and their deep poverty abounded unto the riches of their liberality. For to their power, I bear record, yea, and beyond their power they were willing of themselves; praying us with much intreaty that we would receive the gift, and take upon us the fellowship of the ministering to the saints" (2 Corinthians 8:2-4).

"He which soweth sparingly shall reap also sparingly; and he which soweth bountifully shall reap also bountifully" (2 Corinthians 9:6). These words of Paul prove so true in the spiritual realm. Giving to the service of Christ is a spiritual service. It is rewarded by spiritual things. Paul said that "the administration of this service" (of giving) accomplished two things: (1) It "supplieth the want of the saints." (2) "By the experiment of this ministration they glorify God for your professed subjection unto the gospel of Christ" (2 Corinthians 9:12, 13).

The church lacks finance because the "administration of this service" of giving is not accomplished. God has not changed. If believers would only give as the Word of God directs, the unreceivable blessing promised through Malachi would be theirs. The support of the church and all her enterprises would be met. The support of the poor would be accomplished by the church rather than socialistic government agencies. All the benevolent work undertaken in the name of Christ through the church would be sufficiently financed.

Loyalty to the church should be an expression of one's loyalty to Christ. It is possible to confuse the two, but this should not be true. The church is Christ's means for accomplishing His mission in the world. As we become loyal to the church, we should allow it to express our loyalty to Him. A gift to the church should in reality be a gift to Christ. All our church attendance and gifts should be motivated by a love for Christ.

V. THE WATCHCARE OVER BELIEVERS
(Galatians 6:1-10)

"Am I my brother's keeper?" was not an isolated question asked by a haunted mind six thousand years ago. It is a question which continues to resound. The Church Covenant of Free Will Baptists makes it evident that there is a bond between believers which permits the watchcare, or demands this concern, for each other. The Covenant is reversed to say that "We agree to accept Christian admonition and reproof." It is not difficult to reprove others. In fact, some people delight in it. Oddly enough, it is sometimes the great reprover who cannot accept correction himself.

The Church Covenant places the emphasis on the proper point. If it told us to "admonish and reprove" others, it would go against the biblical admonitions which urge us to "judge not." Care has to be exercised lest we become judges. It is our attitude that we must watch when we are reproved. No one likes reproof. It is natural to resent it. But the believer should take admonition and reproof "with meekness." Even though we may not agree with our corrector, it is our duty to hear his reproof, examine ourselves, and weigh his words carefully.

Several other pledges are also included in this paragraph related to this thought. Notice each of them:

1. "To watch over one another in love." Paul told us to "Owe no man any thing, but to love one another." The Christian should guard his life so that he becomes in no way obligated to man except to love him. Love is the fulfilling of the law of Christ. Watchcare motivated by love seeks the best interests of the one loved. This admonition is completed with the words, "endeavoring to 'keep the unity of the Spirit' in the bonds of peace." Our watchcare and careful attention for each other should be of a nature to ensure peace in the body of Christ.

2. "To be careful of one another's happiness and reputation." When we love someone, we will disbelieve gossip and idle talk about them. We will deny and try to hush up any rumors about them. The love that compels this should permeate the whole body of Christ.

3. "Seek to strengthen the weak, encourage the afflicted, admonish the erring, and . . . promote the success of the church and of the Gospel." Paul taught us to "Bear ye one another's burdens" (Galatians 6:2). The ones overtaken with fault, we are to restore (6:1). As we have opportunity, "Let us do good unto all men" (6:10). The believer should take it as his mission to do all the good he can in every realm he can as often as he can.

VI. THE EXTENSION OF THE KINGDOM
(Colossians 1:1-8)

The last words of the pledge in the previous paragraph leads into this one. As we seek to "promote the success of the church and of the Gospel," we will do the things outlined in this sixth paragraph. Three things are here emphasized:

1. "We will everywhere hold Christian principle sacred and Christian obligations and enterprises supreme." This would fulfill the admonition of Christ who urged us to "Seek ye first the kingdom of God, and his righteousness; and all these things shall be added unto you" (Matthew 6:33). The ethics of Christ and moral standards of Christ set forth in the Sermon on the Mount were intended for believers in our time. Our chief obligations in life are spiritual and not physical and material.

Paul wrote in Colossians 1:1-8 of the "saints" whom he called "faithful brethren." They were this because they were dominated by "faith" in action (verse 4), "love" (verse 4), and "hope" (verse 5). These things in their lives produced "fruit" (verse 6). Our faith, love, and hope also will be demonstrated to the world when we hold our Christian obligations in the supreme place in our lives.

2. "Counting it our chief business in life to extend the influence of Christ in society." Can you imagine every church member dedicated to extending the influence of Christ in society? The early church was dominated by such an attitude. Persecuted, they went everywhere preaching the gospel. Like Paul, they counted all things but loss for Christ.

The Great Commission obligates believers to "every creature" in "all the world." Sometimes we overlook possibilities nearest us. The gospel of Christ can change the life of the neighbor who is a drunkard or the man down the street who is a thief. We are to involve ourselves in every area of society to influence it. Did not Christ describe us as "the light of the world," the "salt of the earth"?

3. "Constantly praying and toiling that the kingdom of God may come, and His will be done on earth as it is in heaven." There are no vacations in one's Christian experience. There are no furloughs from the army of the Lord. The believer is to "be instant in season, out of season" (2 Timothy 4:2). Paul in his extreme situation could see Heaven and being with Jesus as a great release, but he realized that to remain in the world was more needful for the kingdom of God.

The best way for each believer to contribute toward His will being done on earth as it is in Heaven is to find God's will for his own life. Each believer is obligated to find God's will for his life. That will of God in a life will contribute toward achieving God's purposes.

VII. THE SUPPORT OF DENOMINATIONAL ENTER-PRISES
(Philippians 4:2; Romans 16:1, 2; Titus 3:13)

A denomination is made up of people who adhere to a similar interpretation of God's Word. When a group of believers join together to form a denomination, their beliefs lead them to adopt common and cooperative goals. This is true in the Free Will Baptist denomination. Together we cooperate in "educational and denominational enterprises." Included in these are "the support of missions, the success of Sunday schools, and evangelistic efforts for the salvation of the world."

All of these enterprises are planned to promote the one common cause: the salvation of souls. Single churches cannot build a college, publish its own literature, send out missionaries, or promote great extensions of the kingdom. Our local, state, and national associations are set up as cooperative efforts to achieve these larger goals.

The important thing for local members to realize is the vital role that each individual plays in the success of these undertakings. A missionary to India can stay on the field because individual members contribute toward his support. Our Bible colleges can remain open and sustain their work as local members take an interest in their support. Free Will Baptists have not been blessed by great gifts of charity which enable them to undertake the building of large schools. But the faithful gifts of our members have enabled us to build colleges that will meet our needs for training.

Paul and his evangelistic party were able to enter many new areas because they had the support of churches such as those in Macedonia. The needs of the churches in Palestine were met through the contributions of churches established by Paul in his missionary travels. Such common undertakings were begun in the New Testament Church and continue to this day.

The closing words of the Covenant are a prayer that "the God of peace sanctify us wholly, and preserve us blameless unto the coming of our Lord Jesus Christ." The "sanctify us wholly" does not refer to complete sanctification in this life. Free Will Baptists believe in progressive sanctification after the initial sanctification in the new birth which sets us apart for God's use. It is only as we come into His eternal presence that we are sanctified wholly or completely.

The purpose of this Covenant is to bind us together in mutual efforts to perfect His will in our lives and to have us ready at His coming. We need to "keep this commandment without spot, unrebukeable, until the appearing of our Lord Jesus Christ" (1 Timothy 6:14). Since Satan "as a roaring lion, walketh about, seeking whom he may devour" (1 Peter 5:8), it is best for believers to be fortified through mutual strength to resist him.

Chapter Thirteen

Chapter Thirteen

CPSIA information can be obtained at www.ICGtesting.com
Printed in the USA
LVOW07s2351170316

479691LV00001B/1/P

9 780892 650194